MW01235190

RougH
AS A
CoB

BTO Rocks!

ROUGH
AS A
COB

MORE FROM THE
JULIETTE JOURNALS

ED WILLIAMS

RIVER CITY PUBLISHING
Montgomery, Alabama

Published in the United States by River City Publishing,
1719 Mulberry St., Montgomery, AL 36106.

Printed in the United States.
Designed by Nancy Stevens.

Library of Congress Cataloging-in-Publication Data:
Williams, Ed, 1956-
Rough as a cob: more from the Juliette journals / Ed Williams.
p. cm.
ISBN 1-57966-037-1 (hardcover)
1. Williams, Ed, 1956- 2. Georgia-Social life and customs-20th
century-Anecdotes. 3. Georgia-Biography-Anecdotes. I. Title.
CT275.W5654A3 2003
975.8'563043'092-dc21

2003000218

To Big Annie, wherever she may be . . .

CONTENTS

Foreword ...9

Preface ...11

Acknowledgments ...13

Chapter 1   On Being Southern ...15

Chapter 2   Shootin' Down the UFO ...19

Chapter 3   Snake In The Cobs! ...25

Chapter 4   Listen, Listen, The Cat Is Pissin'! ...36

Chapter 5   Ed Sr. ...46

Chapter 6   The Sanctity of the Super Bowl ...61

Chapter 7   Rasslin' and Riskin' (Our Asses) ...66

Chapter 8   Let's Be Honest About Little League ...87

Chapter 9   Odds, Sods, and Clods ...98

Chapter 10   Meetin' BTO ...122

Epilogue ...149

FOREWORD

In the years I've played in BTO, I've had chances to visit lots of different places. I've met tons of people, and have enjoyed the variety of experiences I've encountered. A short while back I came upon this book called *Sex, Dead Dogs, and Me—the Juliette Journals*. I read it, and quickly learned the following things:

1. Country boys from Juliette, Georgia, do some crazy things.

2. Country boys from Juliette, Georgia, have damn good taste in rock 'n' roll music.

On account of this book, Ed Williams and I have become friends. We come from different places, eat different foods, and talk with different accents, but we're friends nonetheless. Friends to the point that all of us guys in BTO are now honorary members of the Brotherhood—it just doesn't get much better than that.

Now, let's get to the point—buy this book. Don't waste another second—buy it. If you don't, I promise you that BTO will never play any of our hits for you again. All you'll get from us are covers of Perry Como stuff. None of us want that now, do we? Buy the book.

Robin Bachman
MARCH 2002

9

PREFACE

Man, if luck was money I'd be Howard Hughes right now. I never would have anticipated that y'all would have wanted to read old stories about Juliette and some of the crazy goings-on in my life. I wrote the first book as nothing more than something that I thought Ed Jr. and the Brotherhood would get a kick out of. What has happened since then has been an amazement to me. Don't get me wrong—I appreciate the hell out of y'all buying and reading *Sex, Dead Dogs, and Me*. I'm equally appreciative that you've bought this book and are about to read it as well. It still surprises me a lot, though.

I really didn't think I'd tackle another book, but I enjoyed writing the first one so much that I'm gonna take a stab at it. I've received lots of letters from people who seem to want more stories and commentary from the big city of Juliette. I've also got a publisher who seems to want more. Hey, who am I to argue? I'll give it to ya.

Acknowledgments

I'd like to thank John Millard Greene, Jr., whom I didn't know at all, but who touched my life just the same. And recognition goes to these people, who've gone beyond the call for me, which will be forever appreciated : The Brotherhood (Ray Pippin, Hugh Foskey), Ed Jr., BTO (Robbie Bachman, Fred Turner, Blair Thornton, and Randy Murray), Jan Janvier, Linda Bleser, Kelli Hyde, Cliff Howard, Ed Grisamore, Kelly Milner Halls, Connie Roberts, Ashley Gordon, Tangela Parker, Nancy Stevens, Steve Lowery, Carolyn and Al Newman, Randy and Spiff, Kay Taylor Parker, Keith Giddeon, Alex Gregory, Jackie K. Cooper, Sandra Okamoto, Glenn Hibberts, Jennifer Sinclair, St. John Flynn, Charlie Deaton, Cheryl Pounds, and Gordon Long.

Finally, thanks go to my spouse and children, who've encouraged me as I've led this crazy life these past few years.

CHAPTER 1
ON BEING SOUTHERN

When certain people tell you they're
not from Georgia, it explains a lot.
— Cliff Howard, a proud, lifelong Georgian

I've read countless pieces over the years about what life is supposed to be like in the South. Or what living here is like. Or what being in the South feels like. Some have deemed it living "the Southern experience" (whatever the hell that is). Some discuss it as if we live in a barren, poverty-stricken cesspool. And a precious few (fortunately for those of us who have to explain our Southern heritage to others at times) describe it as if all of us live in a Beverly Hillbillies-type world (I wouldn't mind having Jed's money, but the reality is that rural Southern mountain people are basic, honest, hardworking people—traits that should be honored instead of ridiculed). All in all, it seems that literature regarding life in the South runs the gamut in terms of descriptiveness, content, and characterization of life.

They are all wrong, you know. Some do get remotely in the ballpark; some wouldn't know what the South is even if a dirt dauber nipped their asses. Nothing is wrong with these writers being interested in us, or how we live, or what we do. It just seems to me that to understand the South you have to get the perspective from a true Southerner.

I fit the bill. I'm a full-blooded, genetic Southerner. I'm very proud to hail from the South and especially proud to live in Georgia, the greatest of all Southern states. I thank God at least once or twice each day for being allowed to live here, usually early when I'm spooning grits or late when I'm reflecting on the day's events. And because of that strong inner feeling, I'd like to take a few minutes and discuss what life here is all about, so that you'll understand what being a Southerner really means.

Being a Southerner means that you honor your mama and daddy. You know intuitively that they love you, want the best for you, and work their asses off for you each day. You love the sound of your mama's voice as much as you do the air you breathe. You try hard to grow up and be the kind of man your father will be proud of—a good man, with just enough piss and vinegar inside to make you interesting to other people. Your dad teaches you that those kind of people succeed in life, which is what he wants for you more than anything in the world—for you to succeed.

You dress up for Sunday school, even though you'd rather swallow insects than do it, 'cause it makes your mother smile. Making her proud of you becomes one of the greatest compulsions in your life. You want her to know how much you love her, and how great it feels to have done something that makes her proud of you. You discover that there is no greater achievement than honoring her by your actions and deeds.

You pass through life speaking slowly, with a drawl, knowing that the slowness of your speech conveys warmth and respect for the listener. If you really think about it, when Southern people speak, our audience actually gets to hear and understand the words we say. And we really don't care if we are mocked for our drawls. That's because we understand that our mockers are usually smart-assed Northerners who don't have a clue as to why we communicate in the verbal manner we do. So we ignore their taunts, or laugh them off, and just keep moving forward. Inner dignity drives our lack of overt response.

You love hearing a football being kicked off a tee at eight o'clock on a Friday night at Mitchell Field in Forsyth (or in countless other high school football palaces in the South). You root like hell for your team to win, but you respect the other team if they do happen to beat you (unless, of course, it's the Jackson Red Devils). You find yourself buying concessions, not out of hunger, but because you know the money you spend helps support the school and keeps those players and cheerleaders working hard each Friday night.

As a young boy you swim in an old pond that is getting drained, covering yourself in mud and laughing at how good it feels. You fling large gobs of mud at bystanders who are not enlightened enough to be in there with you. You enjoy it when your aim is true, and the resultant curses that ring out from your accuracy.

When you reach your teenage years, you find yourself in a cow pasture one evening dumping fresh cow pies into a brown paper bag. After doing this, you go and set them on someone's porch on a dark, Halloween night. You then take a match, light the bag, ring the doorbell quickly, and scram. If you're lucky and turn around at the right point as you run off, you get to see the person who answers the doorbell stomp that fire out.

You stand and proudly salute the Stars and Stripes while shedding an inward tear for your ancestors who fought and died in the Civil War, knowing they were fighting for a cause they believed in. And you wonder, given how history has worked out, if the South wouldn't have been better off to have been allowed its freedom, and the sacred right to choose its own destiny.

You run with the Brotherhood, or your personal equivalent of the Brotherhood (we all know there is no real equivalent, but I'm just saying this to make the rest of you feel good). You understand that best friends can be closer than brothers, and that the adventures all of you have together will be among the most cherished of your life.

One of your favorite movies is *Forrest Gump* because you understand that Forrest figured something out that most of us never do—you unconditionally love the people closest to you. The four people who meant something to him in his life—his mama, Lieutenant Dan, Bubba, and Jenny—had his unconditional love and support. You understand that you should do the same thing in your own life, and you strive like hell to do so.

You stand at attention and with respect when you pass a cemetery containing war veterans' graves. If you walk into the cemetery, you make damn sure you don't step upon the burial sites, and, if any memorials are found overturned, you sit them back upright.

You smile at the heaven brought to your ears by Southern boys like Elvis, Jerry Lee Lewis, and Buddy Holly. You forgive them their earthly flaws, as you know the joy and satisfaction they bring others more than compensate for them. You also know that they loved their mamas, and, in the final analysis, were basically good boys who were blessed with talent from God.

You chomp down on a cold slice of watermelon, watching the juice drip all over you, and not giving a damn about it. You can't let anyone see you give a damn anyway, as your masculinity will get questioned if you eat it in a civilized way (using utensils, for example). For preservation of dignity, you have to jam it down in big chunks—that's how a Southern man eats a melon.

You laugh like hell when you hear Dog tell a story he really shouldn't have at a family gathering. You hold your macho words and jokes back when your mom or wife passes by, and she smiles knowingly at the group. She still knows you love and respect her. And you know that your ass will get lovingly chewed for these particular sins later on.

You pull over when you see a lady with a flat tire and help her. You ask nothing for the effort, as she could be your wife, daughter, or grand-daughter. Her smile and grateful eyes are all the reward you will ever need.

You feel tears well up as you sit at the laser show at Stone Mountain Park and hear Elvis's voice sing, "An American Trilogy." Southerners, if you polled them, would tell you this song is really our national anthem. No one I've ever known, from Velma to Ed Jr., hears this song without pausing and listening to it with both reverence and respect.

You stand up when the preacher says the last words over your mama's casket as you file out of the church to go bury her in the family ceme-tery. The tears come, but you fight to hold them in. You know she would expect you to be a good man and would want you to let her go to her final reward with dignity. You wish you'd had the inner strength to tell her while she lived how much you loved her, and how much she meant to you. You resolve to live out your life to make her proud, and you want very badly to believe you'll be with her again in the hereafter.

All these things, and more, make you a Southerner. The region, its beauty, and the inner dignity of its people have captivated me my entire life. I could yell it from the roof tops, "I'm a Southern boy and damn proud to be." 'Cause I am. And always will be. And when the dust ulti-mately settles, all I can tell you is that I love living in the South and will never leave it. Not for anything or anyone or any amount of money. The bottom line? Some things don't have a price—what you are, being the most important of them.

Chapter 2
SHOOTIN' DOWN THE UFO

Poor ol' God
gets blamed for a lot of things.
— Mark Vinson, Dry Branch philosopher extraordinaire

One thing Ed Jr. maintained throughout my growing up years was the fact that there are just some things in life that we're not meant to understand. Things like why a frog would eat shotgun pellets or why he had to visit my mom's relatives or whatever. He just accepted, without question, that there were some things in life that could never be figured out. That being the case, he reckoned that you had to get on with life and accept those things as they were. Life was just too damn short, he said, to ruin it with thinkin' sometimes.

This mindset explained Ed Jr.'s take on extraterrestrial phenomena such as UFOs. He personally had no doubts that UFOs existed. In fact, it was his opinion that a person was extraordinarily stupid if he thought that we here on earth were the only intelligent beings around. As he so often told us, "There's an ass of stars out there. Only a damn fool would believe that there ain't one or two with planets that have intelligent life on 'em. Hell, even a piss ant could reason that out."

All this logic didn't really mean much to a ten-year-old boy in the summer of 1966. UFOs or flying saucers were something that thrilled you in the movies, not something that you'd have to deal with in real life. Little did I know that I was soon to experience a close encounter of a very different kind.

In August of '66 my brother Ernest and I were playing catch in our front yard. It was a sunny afternoon and we both loved to play ball—we would throw each other grounders, pop-flies, and line drives for hours on end. Often we would pretend to be the pitcher and catcher in the World Series. We had all sorts of signs worked up for our different pitches and would even slip a spitter or two into our repertoire.

One day we were throwing the ball around when my brother angled a high, lazy fly ball into the air. I circled around under it to make the catch. As I did, I noticed a faint glint as the ball fell and popped into my glove. Squinting from the glare, I shielded my eyes and looked up, trying to see what in the hell that glint was.

The glare was from something silver and oblong shaped. It resembled a shiny silver cigar floating around in the sky. Whatever it was, it was scary. As Brother looked up, the object seemed motionless and then—it moved! Our eyes got real wide when that happened.

"What in the devil is it?" Brother asked.

I replied that I didn't know, but Ed Jr. was sure to. Thinking I'd better tell him what was going on, I ran into our house to locate him. I found him sitting in his favorite chair in the den. He was propped up reading the paper, his belt undone, and his pants partially unzipped. He was also cussing President Johnson (as usual) pretty intently.

"I'd trust a damn numbers runner before I'd trust his ass!" bellowed Ed Jr. as he recited from the article he was reading. Apparently the president had ordered some spending over in Europe for something my dad didn't quite agree with. Whenever something like this happened, Ed Jr. would read the article aloud and then add his commentary (those commentaries alone, captured on paper, would make a great book). He was about to continue insulting President Johnson some more when he looked up and saw me.

"What do you want, Al (his nickname for me)?" he asked.

"Dad, you're not gonna believe what's up in the sky!" I stammered back.

"Well, what is it?" he asked.

"Please, just get up and come out into the front yard right now!"

Ed Jr. looked sorta funny but stood up and sat his paper in his chair. Then he tightened his belt, zipped his britches (for those of you wondering why they were unzipped, Ed Jr. always loosened his belt and unzipped his britches when he sat down to eat or relax. When asked why he did this, he answered that a man needed room for some things and that he was an American), and walked on out into our front yard. I followed closely at his heels.

As he made his way outside, my brother Ernest ran up to him and pointed into the sky. What the three of us saw made us gasp.

The cigar-shaped object was now round and had moved several hundred feet! Brother and I were astonished but Ed Jr. had as serious a look going on his face as I have ever seen. His jaw muscles were clenched and it looked like most of the color had drained from his face. He kept staring until I broke the silence.

"Sure is interesting. Ain't it, Dad?" I intoned.

"Interesting ain't the damn word, boy. I've read about 'em, seen pictures of 'em, but now . . ."

Ed Jr. stopped and turned towards the house. Then, with no further comments, he starting running. Running as fast as he possibly could. The front door swung open mightily when he entered and slammed just as quickly behind him as he vanished inside.

Ernest and I stared at each other in complete amazement. We'd never seen the old man move like that before. Sure, he'd cuss the Braves and Falcons, and he'd get pretty animated when any Democrat phoned him seeking his vote, but this sprint to the house was totally out of the ordinary. We both just stood there for awhile, unsure as to what to make of all this.

Before our minds had much of a chance of deciphering these events, the front door flew open again and Ed Jr. was coming back outside. He was walking very fast and had the biggest shotgun that he owned in his hands. His eyes were like slits and he looked like someone who had just joined a religious cult or, worse yet, had won a free weekend trip at a timeshare vacation joint.

As he came up on Brother and me, my mind was doing mental cartwheels. I was always an inquisitive-type kid and I was dying to find out exactly what Ed Jr. was gonna do with that shotgun. The only thing was, common sense dictated that now was not the time to ply the old man with questions. Hell, we didn't know what sort of spell he was under. Brother and I didn't think he was gonna shoot us or anything, but there was no point in testing that assumption.

Ed Jr. took his shotgun and pointed it towards the sky. Brother and I immediately took several steps back. We were both pretty frightened and then it finally dawned on us—he was gonna try to shoot the UFO down with his shotgun! I couldn't believe that he would try to do that! I immediately blurted out, "You can't be serious about trying to hit that thing."

"Damn right I'm gonna try to hit it. Why in the hell do you think I brought this gun out here?"

"Dad, that thing looks like it's really high up there in the sky."

We all looked up together after I said that. The funny thing being that we didn't have a clue as to how high up the object really was. For an instant it would look like it was ten miles up, then it would appear to be much closer to the ground. After observing this phenomenon for a few minutes, Ed Jr. had the mystery solved.

"Those alien bastards are accelerating up and down in the sky! They're getting close and then flying straight up—damn their asses!" he exclaimed.

I swear Ed Jr. felt that the extraterrestrial pilots of this UFO were teasing him—challenging him to see whether or not he would pull the trigger, putting a moving target in front of him just to tempt him. I can remember watching him and seeing the veins in his neck standing up over this perceived insult. Brother and I both wondered just where all this was leading when BLAM! Ed Jr. had fired upon the spacecraft! Brother and I looked upwards, hoping to see a wounded spaceship that was trailing debris and smoke and headed straight towards the ground. What we saw was an unhit UFO that seemed to have moved just a tad to the right.

Ed Jr. interpreted this slight movement to mean that the UFO pilots had barely avoided his shot. He quickly reloaded and bore down yet again on the alien intruder.

BLAM! This shot seemed even louder than the first. We all looked up, waiting to see if any damage had been done to the spacecraft. After a few seconds it was obvious that none had been inflicted, and the UFO was still hovering around just as before.

Ernest spoke up and said, "It's up there too high, Dad! You ain't ever gonna hit it."

Those words poured more gasoline on the already raging fire within Ed Jr. First off, this damn spaceship was playing a candy-assed game of cat-and-mouse with him. Secondly, he had to hear his own sons express doubts as to what he was doing. Finally, all this frustration came to bear on him and caused him to stop looking up at the sky. He shifted his gaze, and then glared over at my brother and me. As usual, he didn't hesitate to let us know what exactly was on his mind.

"You know, you little shits will never amount to anything lookin' at things the way you do! How will we ever know whether or not this damn spaceship can be shot down unless we try?" When a few seconds went by, and he got no answer to his question, he super-glared at us and asked, "Well?"

Neither one of us could answer him. Brother and I felt at this point that the best thing to do was assure Ed Jr. that he was on the right path and that we were both solidly in his corner. We thusly perjured ourselves, he seemed pleased with our newly improved attitudes, and then it was back to serious business.

BLAM! Shots three, four, five, and six were fired off in rapid succession. The thing was, the object never moved an inch during the barrage.

Finally, after firing off the last couple of blasts, Ed Jr. was convinced that the object was just too high up in the sky.

The fact that he had fired off all these shots didn't bother him at all. As he put it, "Well, the way I see it, Columbus took some helluva risks. People told him he was gonna sail off the corner of the world. Told him he wouldn't find anything." When Brother and I asked him just what had caused Columbus to go ahead and sail anyway, the old man explained, "Look, Columbus just had a damn itch to see if there was a new world. He probably thought about it a lot and got damn tired of thinkin' about it. When you get to that point boy, there's only one thing you can do. Find out for yourself—blaze the damn trail! That's what I did with this UFO. I blazed the damn trail!" When I interjected that it was all for naught he said, "And why? If I'd hit the damn thing, y'all's tongues would be hanging out so far they'd be tickling a snail's ass now!"

I had to admit that he had me there. I admired his "willing to take on the world" attitude, even in the face of an alien invader. This obviously was not a man who approached life in a typical manner. This was a man who seemed to feel he could mold events to his liking and was adamant about not letting destiny shape him—Ed Jr. was going to shape his own destiny. I was impressed with his resolve; it seemed incredibly powerful to a ten-year-old boy.

During the next couple of days a story appeared in the local newspaper. An experimental weather balloon out of Florida had gotten loose a couple of days earlier and had drifted over into the skies of central Georgia. Because of its construction, the winds changed its shape quite easily. The paper also reported that local police and civil defense stations had been swamped with calls about this strange object. Many people were convinced that they had seen a UFO and, in some cases, were panicking.

I handed the paper over to Ed Jr. and pointed out the story. He read it over carefully, the scowl on his face growing as he made his way through the lines. He then tossed the paper to one side.

"Dammit, I thought I had really seen a UFO," he said. He said the odds, of course, were always that the object was explainable, but he didn't know that when he saw it. He had to take action right then, lest the opportunity be lost. He then paused, thought some more, and added, "I hope to hell that you'll have the balls to take initiative in life like I did. Life rewards those who show some gumption and who are willing to roll the dice at times! What a damn story it woulda been if I'd shot that thing down."

I looked at Ed Jr. and smiled. Then I started laughing. The whole episode was so bizarre, yet funny at the same time. At first Ed Jr. was pissed 'cause I was laughing. After a few moments, though, he smiled and started laughing himself. As he was cackling he said something that I'll never forget, "Well, one thing about it. No one will ever know I shot at the damn thing anyway."

Not exactly . . .

Chapter 3
SNAKE IN THE COBS!

☾

She was movin' faster than a
centipede on a hotplate.
— Uncle Dog

Bathroom equity can lead to some very serious consequences. But I'll bet you haven't a clue as to what bathroom equity is. After you read the tale captured here, you'll understand this term much better. I guarantee it.

Modern bathroom technology hadn't quite made its way into Juliette by the late thirties or early forties. Flush toilets were few and far between, and the outdoor privy was the generally utilized bathroom of the era. Ed Jr. and Dog (that's my uncle Jimmy, for all of you who didn't read the first epistle; I'd suggest buying a copy now, so that you are up to speed for the rest of this book) reminisced often about the hardships of using the outdoor privy.

"It was hell turning up your ass on a cold December morning," Ed Jr. said one evening when he and Dog were about to go to a cockfight. "The wind would come up under the outhouse and sting both cheeks like hornets. And your balls would draw up like curtains when those cold breezes hit them."

Dog added, "The worst thing was havin' to use those damn cobs."

"Corn cobs?" I interrupted. "What did you use corn cobs for?"

Ed Jr. and Dog both looked at each other like I was slightly daft. "Damn, boy. We had to use corn cobs for toilet paper," Ed Jr. explained.

I was amazed at this revelation, but then figured the two of them must be pulling my leg. And I told them so. When I did, Dog immediately launched into a brief history of rural Southern bathroom habits.

"Al, when we were coming up we didn't have it nice and soft like you do now—indoor flush toilets with fancy, scented toilet paper; bathrooms with vents in 'em. In fact, when we came up the only toilet paper you had was a Sears, Roebuck catalogue."

"You hear all that crap now about how everyone back then wanted the Sears Christmas catalogue to look at toys and all. That was a bunch of shit. We always wanted lots of Sears catalogues 'cause it was the only alternative to a cold, frozen cob."

Of course, I laughed like hell at that. When I did, Dog started looking very seriously at me. I took this to mean that he was on a roll and that I should just shut up and listen. And I was right. Dog then went on with this little known facet of Southern history.

"Corn cobs were hell on your ass. But they were all there was, till the Sears, Roebuck catalogues came along. Ed Sr. would take the cobs we had and lay them out back in the sun to dry them. Then they went into a bucket inside the privy."

Dog squinted up at the sun and continued, "A damn cob is rough on its best days. If you sat in a fire ant bed it wouldn't have hurt any worse than using one of them to wipe with. And that was the upside of it. I'm talking about the warm days. In the winter, it got even worse. Let's say a pain hit you around three o'clock in the morning. You'd stagger out of bed and slowly stumble through the house. Once you got to the door and opened it, a blast of cold air would wake you and make your hair almost stand on end. That's 'cause we had to wear these damn sleep gown things back then. They weren't nuthin' but a damn tent and made you feel prissy to boot. Worse thing, though, was when a shot of cold air went up those gowns. It would make your balls go up into your throat and your breath drop down into your stomach."

"Then you'd walk on out in the yard, colder than hell, and your bowels rumbling like a salted snail. Sometimes you'd trot if the pains were bad enough. Then, you'd spy the privy out over in the far corner of the yard.

"You'd walk faster then, 'cause you knew you were close to giving your intestines a good work out. Once you got to the privy, you'd open the door, sit down, and do your business as quickly as you could. Once you'd finished, you'd reach down into that bucket and pull out a cold, wet cob."

Dog looked over at Ed Jr. at this point. Ed Jr. nodded solemnly, and Dog continued onwards with his story.

"You prayed like hell that that cob had been dried out good before the old man dropped it in the bucket. The reason for this was that if the cob hadn't dried out it would freeze. And the only damn thing worse than wiping with a cold cob was wiping with a cold, frozen, ice-filled cob. You'd just about rather have dropped your balls into a steel trap as to use one of those Popsicle cobs."

Ed Jr. chimed in at this point, "See what I mean, boy? You gotta admit, times are better now."

"Well, no shit," I wanted to say, but I felt the words would be an ill-timed pun. Those cobs had to have been hell to use if you gauged the expressions on the faces of Ed Jr. and Dog. I felt that my continued silence was appropriate for their somber tale of cold cobs and chafed skin.

Dog went on to say that in the early to mid 1940s, Ed Sr. and Miss Lily installed the first indoor toilet in Juliette. He said that he and Ed Jr. were beside themselves with joy.

This joy ended, however, soon after the new toilet's installation when Miss Lily and Ed Sr. convened the whole family. Starting with a few words about this wonderful possession, Ed Sr. laid its rules of usage out.

"Boys," Ed Sr. said, "we are all glad about having this new flush toilet in our house. It should make things a lot easier for most of us. It's cleaner and I won't have to dry near as many cobs now."

"Near as many?" asked Ed Jr. "Why will we need any more cobs at all?"

"Because, boy—we all can't use the flush toilet," Ed Sr. sternly replied.

The family was both surprised and bewildered. They got even more solemn when Ed Sr. went on.

"I know y'all won't like this, but the problem is in the mornings. Every one of y'all gets up and the first thing you want to do is take an early morning dump. Why y'all all want to shit in the mornings, I don't know, but you do. Hell, to be straight, even I do it. I just like to get it out of the way before the day starts. And with five boys and a girl we just don't have time for everyone to ascend to the throne before they leave for school."

At this point Uncle Dog chimes up and point-blank asks who will be allowed to use the flush toilet. Ed Sr. answered quickly, "I think the only fair thing to do is make it where your sister always gets to use the flush toilet. She is a girl, you know. Ed, you and Dog are the oldest boys. Y'all are going to have to keep using the privy as you're both tough enough to take it. Plus, y'all both crap like a yard mule. Makes sense for y'all to keep going outside. Never said that life was gonna be easy, boys. But I know you'll support me in this as you have in other things."

Ed Jr. said that he couldn't wait to get outside and cuss. He looked at Dog, and then they both walked outside together. Once outside they began ranting and raving about the inequities involved in this situation. Not being able to use the flush toilet? It was enough to make one's blood dance with the demons.

"That damn Trina. Her ass must be made out of gold or something," Ed Jr. said.

Dog got a serious, Foskey-type look going and said that he was resorting to sabotage. "If I have to, I'll squeeze it back everyday till about noon and come home and use the flush toilet. Just to make things fair! It ain't right that Fee gets to sit on the throne and we have to pull ice splinters out of our asses."

Thus planned, the days went by and, true to his word, Dog went home every day at lunch time and used the flush toilet. His daily routine went off without a hitch for about two to three months until the inevitable snafu occurred.

It seems that one particular day Dog went home at lunch, ate a couple of sandwiches, and then went inside to use the flush toilet. Everything was going okay until he realized, as he sat there, that he had lost track of the time and was late for a history test being given. When he remembered the test, Dog immediately finished his business, jumped up, and flushed the toilet.

There was one problem—in his haste to flush the toilet, Dog pushed the handle down so hard that he broke it off. The whole damn handle. It was so cleanly broken off that there was no way the toilet could be flushed again until the handle was replaced.

Dog broke into a semi-panic knowing just how badly he had screwed up. The only thing was, he had no time to cover his tracks as he was already late for his history test. I guess Dog figured that at this point the only thing worse than breaking the toilet was to both break the toilet and fail the history test. This logic definitely tracks for me. Thus decided, Dog ran out of the house and went back to school.

When school let out for the day and the kids began walking home, Dog grabbed Ed Jr. and pulled him off to the side. He then spilled his guts about what had transpired at lunch time. Ed Jr. laughed like hell at Dog's dilemma, but he realized there was potential for Dog to get his ass really torn up. It wasn't just the fact that he had broken the toilet, but it was also the fact that he was sneaking home and taking clandestine dumps. As Ed Jr. told him, "The old man ain't gonna take kindly to the fact that you've been using the throne, 'specially after he told us not to use it."

Dog admitted he had played hell but still pleaded for help from Ed Jr. The two boys talked for awhile and then agreed that the best strategy was to act dumb and let the whole thing blow over. Don't even let on that anything had happened. Play it totally cool. That way, no one's ass got scorched and life would go on as it normally did.

This having been decided, the two boys calmly walked home. Ed Jr. kept reminding Dog not to have a guilty look on his face and to think through the answers to any questions posed by Ed Sr. before he said them out loud. Dog promised that he would do as instructed. The boys kept on talking till they got close to the house. As they walked up into the driveway they heard these words, "Get your asses in here now!"

These tender words were spoken by Ed Sr., who was replicating the demeanor of a rutting hog. Ed Jr. said that he and Dog shuffled inside the house and saw Ed Sr., Miss Lily, Trina, and his other brothers sitting on the living room floor. Ed Sr. was standing up in the center of the room. "Get in here and sit down," he commanded.

As Ed Sr. was not one to be trifled with, the two boys walked in and immediately sat down. When the room got suitably quiet, Ed Sr. began speaking. "It's a bad thing when a man can't have a working crapper. I came in this afternoon to find that the damn handle has been broken off the flush toilet. I'd be an idiot not to know that someone in here came by this afternoon, took an unauthorized shit, and broke this damn toilet. Now, I want to know who the mystery shitter is."

Ed Jr. said that it got so quiet that you could have heard a pin drop. Ed Sr. asked once again, "Who broke the flush toilet?"

There was silence in the room. Ed Sr. then looked around and said, "Well, if one of you won't fess up, I guess it means an ass beating for everyone in this room. Wolf (Ed Jr. for all you first book nonreaders), get outside behind the barn and drop yer britches."

My dad said that he would rather have eaten dog hair as to have to take the ass broiling, but he just couldn't rat Dog out in this situation. He didn't have to worry about that long, though. Dog wasn't the kind to do that kind of thing to his brother. He piped up and said, "Don't take him out there. I was the one that was strainin' biscuits."

Ed Sr. told Dog that his actions had earned him a trip behind the barn. Out the front door the two of them walked. Ed Jr. remarked that it would have been easier to watch a condemned man go to the chair than have to watch Dog take that long walk to the barn.

Around twenty minutes later, Dog walked upstairs and went into the bedroom he shared with my dad. Ed Jr. said that his cheeks were flushed and that he was rubbing his ass with both hands.

"And all because Fee can't turn her lilywhite up outdoors! We've had everything happen but leopards snap our asses in that privy but we still have to use it. It just ain't fair!" Dog bemoaned.

Ed Jr. agreed with Dog but reminded him that his ass-whupping was history. He then added that all the wailing and moaning in the world wasn't gonna change things. Dog just mumbled and said that it was easy for Ed Jr. to say that but it was his ass that was throbbing. Ed Jr. reminded Dog that that was the price you paid for being the mystery shitter. Gradually, the boys quieted down and went on about their daily routines.

That night, as they went to bed, Dog remarked to Ed Jr., "Tomorrow has got to be a better day."

As the sun rose the next morning, the silence in the house was broken by a plaintive wail coming from the kitchen. "I'm not going to use that outdoor toilet. You'll have to make other arrangements!"

Ed Jr. said that the remark was so loud that it bolted him right up out of the bed. Dog woke up quickly as well and said, "It's Trina!"

Trina was in the kitchen raising hell about having to go outside and use the privy. She implored Miss Lily to drive her to Forsyth so that she could use a "proper toilet." She reminded her that she was her only daughter. This conversation was raging when Dog muttered, "Isn't this a fine sack of crabs?"

Ed Jr. agreed that Trina had definitely been spoiled, but that was the way things were. The boys stopped talking as more of the conversation from the kitchen wafted back into their room. "I am not going out there and you are not going to make me do it!" Trina shouted.

By then even Ed Sr. got a little pissed off. He told Trina that he didn't have time to run her to Forsyth and that she had better get on out to the privy and do her business.

At this point, Dog jumped out of the bed, looked right at Ed Jr., and said, "The snake!"

Ed Jr. said his brain sorta locked up for a second due to the suddenness of the comment. The snake? He knew Dog kept an old garter snake in a shoebox underneath his bed. Was that what he was talking about?

Ed Jr.'s thoughts were interrupted as Dog scrambled underneath his bed and pulled the shoebox out. Sitting on the edge of his bed, he slowly opened the top of the box. As Ed Jr. stepped over and peered into it, the boys saw the little green snake curled up in a corner, peering out as if it were looking towards them.

"Ol' Ropey here is gonna make things right!" Dog exclaimed. Ed Jr. still was unsure as to what Dog had in mind, but before he could ask him, Dog grabbed the box and rushed out the door.

As Dog shinnied his way down the stairs, Ed Jr. continued hearing Trina wail on about her plight in the kitchen. Ed Sr. was firmly informing her that her ass would be tomato red if she didn't get on out to the privy and do what she needed to do. Ed Jr. admitted that this was fun to listen to, but he wanted to find out what Dog was doing. He then walked over to his window and looked out, trying to spot him. It didn't take him long to locate his snake-carrying brother.

Not only was Dog out there, but he was running like a scalded dog towards the privy, shoebox in tow. Ed Jr. said it finally hit him at that point—Dog was gonna put that snake in the corn cob bucket in the outhouse! He said that just the thought of it made him laugh so hard that Ed Sr. hollered upstairs at him, wanting to know what was wrong. Ed Jr. assured him that things had never been more right than they were at that moment. Thus satisfied, Ed Sr. went on back to his debate with Trina.

Even though the outhouse was a distance away from the house, Ed Jr. clearly viewed what Dog was doing (this is not unusual—Ed Jr. is far-sighted and can see traffic signs long before anyone else can). He saw him drop ol' Ropey right down into the cob bucket. Then he noticed Dog removing the two Sears, Roebuck catalogues that were in there. Ed Jr. said that you had to admire the thoroughness Dog was exhibiting— he was leaving nothing to chance in this escapade.

The debate between Ed Sr. and Trina finally drew to a close. My dad said he could hear her walk through the house to the front door, open it, and then go outside. Ed Jr. knew she was making her way out back to the privy. What he feared most was that she would see Dog out there, and the whole scheme would be ruined.

There was nothing to worry about, as events proved. Ol' Dog looked up and saw Trina approaching long before she even glanced towards the outhouse. Instead of running back inside the house, Dog positioned himself behind an oak tree that was real close to the privy. Apparently, he wanted a first-hand view of the tender festivities that were about to occur.

Trina trudged down to the privy, muttering to herself the whole way. Dog said that he nearly blew the whole thing by laughing out loud. He got so tickled that the only way he kept himself from laughing was to bite into a limb of the tree he was hiding behind. "That damn bark was bitter, and for all I knew it was poisonous, but I had to do it. Watching ol' Fee acquainting herself with those cobs was worth a million bucks to me. And, if she got to meet ol' Ropey too . . ."

Trina walked up to the door of the privy, wondering out loud as to how much longer it would be until the flush toilet got fixed. Then, she shut the door and silence reigned.

The silence didn't last long, though. Through the bottom of the outhouse Dog could see the bucket of cobs. He saw Trina's pale white hand reach into the bucket. She withdrew one cob. But nothing eventful happened.

Dog said he had almost given up and left his spot behind the tree when Trina reached down into the bucket for cob number two. She was having a problem getting her fingers wrapped around one of those cobs (Dog and Ed Jr. both said that in the winter they could get pretty slippery). Her hand darted in and out of the bucket repeatedly, trying to secure a cob to allow her to finish her business.

Dog said that he came out from behind the tree and snuck even closer to the outhouse. He got close enough to clearly see Trina's hand in the cob bucket. Dog said that her fingers were moving around like Jerry Lee Lewis's on a keyboard—fast and with purpose. Her fingers moved around that bucket until she accidentally grasped ol' Ropey.

Dog said that Trina squeezed pretty hard, thinking she had finally secured a soft, slick cob. When she did, she looked down and noticed that she had a handful of snake instead. She also noticed Ol' Ropey sinking his tiny fangs well into her wrist.

"AUGH!" came the shriek from Trina's lips. Dog said that it was the loudest cry he had ever heard in his life, short of the time he had sex with a Florida woman and accidentally inserted his member someplace he shouldn't have. He then said that Trina bolted up and sprinted out of the privy, hollering like an about-to-be-investigated politician.

Ed Jr. positioned himself so that he had a real good view of the front of the outhouse. He commented that he had never heard such a loud scream in his life. He said that the door slammed open and Trina flew out across the backyard. What made it even worse was that her britches were down, which caused her to fall several times during her mad dash to the house. It didn't matter to Trina, though. She was so upset that she didn't even notice that she was running across the yard and exposing herself for all the world to see.

Ed Sr. noticed though. He had been out front about to crank up his truck when Trina's first shrieks came from the backyard. He later on said that he thought a covey of wolves must have been snacking on her. I would have given anything to have seen the expression on his face when he ran to the backyard and saw his britches-less daughter running, covered with dirt, and hollering with all the force she could muster.

Dog said that Ed Sr. stopped Trina right in her tracks and told her to pull her britches up. Then Ed Sr. tried to make some sense out of what had just happened. This was hard to do as Trina was blubbering so that it was difficult to understand anything she was saying. As he tried to discover what had just occurred, he heard another sound off in the distance. Before investigating it, he decided that Trina needed to go inside and see Miss Lily about fixing her bumps and bruises.

Ed Sr. walked Trina into the house where Miss Lily was waiting for her in the doorway. Once Miss Lily began attending to her, Ed Sr. walked back outside to where he heard all the "sounds" coming from. They appeared to be coming from just out back behind the privy.

When Ed Sr. walked over to where the sounds were coming from, his suspicions were confirmed. For he saw, right there before his eyes, his own son Dog rolling around on the ground and laughing hysterically. He was laughing so hard that tears were welling up in his eyes. Dog was enjoying himself to such a degree that he didn't even bother to hide his laughter when he saw Ed Sr. standing there before him.

Dog had never been so tickled in his life. He also felt that justice had finally been served in this situation. The only problem he had to face was the fact that he was up to his eyeballs in hot water with Ed Sr. His father's face was an immobile mask as Dog got to his feet, dusted himself off, and waited for his dad's reaction.

Ed Sr. looked at his son for the longest time. Then, he said, in a very low voice, "She deserved it."

Dog said that he couldn't believe what Ed Sr. had just said. But that was not the end of what he had to say.

"She really did deserve it, Dog. After I told you and Wolf (Ed Jr.'s nickname—see, y'all really do need to buy the first book in order to be savvy with the nicknames) that y'all had to keep using the privy, I know it had to rile both of you up. And then to hear Trina complaining like hell this morning? I can understand how y'all felt, having to use icy cobs while Trina was using the flush toilet. She had no right to bitch about that privy at all."

Dog said it was as emotional a moment as he ever had with his old man. They sorta hugged each other and Jimmy felt that the worst was over. Basically it was, except for one minor problem.

"The problem is, if I don't tear your ass up for this I'll never hear the end of it from Miss Lily. She'll think I showed you favoritism. I don't want to do it, but I don't think I have a choice," stated Ed Sr.

Dog said that this really jolted him from his feelings of relief over the situation. Ed Sr. was known to dole out some pretty fierce ass-whuppings. Dog knew that he had to pull this one out of the fire very quickly. Gambling on a long shot, Dog tried the following argument.

"Look, Dad. I think I can go in the house and act like I've had my ass torn up. Hollywood actors do it all the time. If I do a real good job, no one would know and we'd all be happy."

"Boy, if I let you do that, can you make it look real?" Ed Sr. asked.

"Dad, given the choice between acting like I got my ass torn up, and having to get my ass torn up, what would you do if you was me?" Dog queried back.

Ed Sr. decided to try Dog's idea. Jimmy said the first thing he did when he got the green light was to let himself laugh real hard to get a good teary eyed look going. Then, Ed Sr. grabbed him by the arm and marched him into the house.

Upon entering the front door, Ed Sr. called out, "Lily, come here dammit." Miss Lily dutifully came down the stairs, walked into the front room, and saw her husband and super—remorseful son standing there before her.

"Tell her what you have to say, boy," Ed Sr. demanded.

"Mama, I put that snake in the cob bucket. It was my fault. And Daddy has just torn my ass up for it!"

Dog said that it took all the willpower he could muster to look serious as he delivered those lines. But the stakes were too high to mess things up. If he didn't come through, Ed Sr. would have been embarrassed as hell. That would have meant he would have received an ass-whupping double in scope to the one than he would have gotten in the first place.

Miss Lily told Dog how disappointed she was in him, but added that he appeared to have been punished sufficiently for his misstep. She told him that the last thing he had to do to atone for things was to go apologize to Trina for what he did.

Dog walked into the den and saw Trina sitting on the sofa. Her hand was wrapped up with about twenty pounds of bandages and her eyes were still swollen from crying so hard. Dog walked over to his sister and said, "Fee, I'm sorry for throwing that snake in the cob bucket."

Trina looked up at Dog and told him that he should be ashamed of himself. Dog quickly replied, "Hey, I said I was sorry. I've suffered here, too. I've gotten my ass torn up and my pet snake is dead 'cause you squeezed him so hard."

"That snake deserves to be dead for what he did! And you had better not scare me like that again," Trina hollered.

Dog said that he just nodded at her and walked out of the room. He went upstairs and, after swearing Ed Jr. to secrecy, cued him in on the whole story. Ed Jr. told him that they could never tell anyone about this until they were grown or both of them would get their asses torn up. And this is exactly what they did until they both did grow up and then told me this story. I didn't realize it at the time but I was the first person they had told it to in all these years. And, to be frank, I have never told it to another person until now. It is such a good story that I really think Dog, Ed Sr., and Miss Lily would enjoy knowing that it had gotten out and had brought people pleasure.

Bathroom equity—now y'all know what it is and why it can be such a disruptive force. All the readers of this book should now, in a show of solidarity, hang a dried cob from a rope tied to a tree in their yard to show their sensitivity to this politically correct concept. Before you know it, cobs will be hanging from trees everywhere in America. And this could come in real handy if any of us Williamses ever need to make a quick pit stop somewhere.

Chapter 4
"LISTEN, LISTEN...
THE CAT IS PISSIN'!"

☾

Poems are like doilies
—no man ever admits that he likes 'em.
— Ed Jr.

I've gotta be honest with y'all here—I've never been a big poetry fan. Not to be rude, but I always saw people who wrote poetry as being a little light in the loafers. It seemed to me that anyone could string some rhythmic verse together (and yes, I do know there are other forms of poetry, but they suck just as much, too) and call themselves poets. Hell, I'll bet that right this second I can just throw one together on a whim. Watch this:

Her hair was nice,

But her butt was big,

As she ate, she snorted,

Was she woman, or pig?

See? This is obviously not a great poem, but I still knocked it out in about twenty seconds. Big deal, huh? Suffice it to say that I'm not as appreciative of poetry as some people are.

It's not just a feeling I have. The entire Brotherhood feels the same way. In fact, when I mentioned to Hugh and Ray that I would be writing a chapter involving poetry, they both looked at me strangely and muttered something about revocation of my Brotherhood membership. In our world, masculinity and poetry just don't walk hand in hand.

Imagine how startled Hugh and Ray were when I told them that one of the great unsung poets in American literary history is Ed Jr.! That's right—Ed Jr. I know that, based upon what I have written about him in the past, some of you out there may find that somewhat surprising (in fact, damn surprising). But, Ed Jr. has composed many poems over the years, some of which are destined to be future American literary classics.

My exposure to them began when I was about three or four years of age. At an age where most kids are busily learning Mother Goose rhymes, Ed Jr. was exposing me to rhymes of a different sort.

I vividly remember my first Ed Jr. poetry recitation one afternoon as I was watching him feed the chickens. As he tossed feed to them, I heard him say, "Listen, listen, the cat is pissin'."

I liked how those words rhymed and asked him to repeat them again. He did, and even told me that when you made words rhyme like that it was called a poem. He said that when you added music to a poem that it became a song. It made perfect sense to me.

A couple of years later I was in elementary school and learning some of the standard nursery rhymes that you would expect a young child to pick up. I discovered that Ed Jr.'s poetry was a little different from the norm.

Mrs. Bennett was my first grade teacher. She was a nice, middle-aged lady who appeared to love teaching. On the day in question, Mrs. Bennett was reading us Mother Goose rhymes.

After reading several of them, Mrs. Bennett told us how she loved rhymes and poems. She spent time explaining to us what a poem really was. After that, she looked out and asked if any of us knew rhymes that we would share with the class.

A few of my classmates stood up and recited little poems that their parents had taught them about God, or life, or whatever. Mrs. Bennett nodded approvingly at them. James Sapp, who sat right behind me, recited a poem about horses in a pasture that ate candy hay, or something ridiculous like that. When he finally sat down, Mrs. Bennett asked if anyone else knew of a poem that they would like to share with the class.

At this moment James, being the sneaky little shit that he was, jabbed me in the rib cage with his finger. This caused me to jump straight up out of my seat and make a gasping sound. When I did, Mrs. Bennett was on me like a panther. I can vividly remember her saying, "Oh Edward, do you have a poem you'd like to share with the class?"

You might not know it by the way I act now, but I was painfully withdrawn when I was a child. It would've killed me to have to stand up and recite a poem in front of the whole class. But I also knew that you respected your teacher, and when she called on me I felt like I was obligated to quote some kind of poem.

I stood beside my desk, my heart pounding like a BTO drum riff. My mind was frozen because I was so nervous. I couldn't think of one single poem. The pressure got even worse when Mrs. Bennett asked me if I was serious about reciting a poem.

"Yes, ma'am. I am. I know one I can say."

"Then, Edward, by all means recite it," answered Mrs. Bennett.

I was so terrified at this point that only one poem came to mind. "Listen, listen, the cat is pissin'."

The room was quiet for a split second. Then bursts of laughter exploded that I still remember. The kids in my class were hanging out of their desks laughing, literally rolling in the aisles.

As for me, I was embarrassed as hell. It made it even worse when I could tell that Mrs. Bennett didn't like my poem. She looked me dead in the eye and asked me where I had learned it. I told her in a clear voice that my father had taught it to me. I also added that it was one of his favorite poems. Mrs. Bennett got a really flushed look on her face. She seemed to be getting quite angry as well.

Mrs. Bennett walked to her desk and scribbled on a sheet of stationery. She wrote furiously for awhile, looking up at me every now and then. When she finished, she stuck her message into an envelope and put Ed Jr.'s name on the outside. She got up from her desk, walked over, and handed me the envelope. She said, "Edward, I want you to take that note to your father and tell him I expect an answer."

I told Mrs. Bennett that I would do as she asked.

I was a total wreck the rest of the day. I wanted so badly to open that envelope and see what kind of message Mrs. Bennett had written to my father. Was she telling him I was bad? A degenerate poem reader? I really didn't have a clue, but I would not have dared open that envelope. I figured that the best thing to do was take it home, but have a good speech prepared for my dad to preface things with. Then I would present him with the note.

The school day ended and I got on the bus going home. I thought and thought and finally came up with the appropriate speech. The general idea was that I was going to hold my breath a lot right before I got to the house, in order to work up a good "flushed" facial expression. I would then present Mrs. Bennett's note to Ed Jr., but act and appear really "out of it." I figured that he might think that I was sick with a fever or something, and not hold me accountable for my actions at school earlier that day.

The bus finally pulled up in front of my house. To tell you the truth, I got off it pretty winded as I had held my breath intermittently for the last ten or so minutes of the ride. I walked up my driveway, then sort of staggered into the house.

Ed Jr. happened to be sitting at the kitchen table when I walked in. He was reading the newspaper and giving President Kennedy a pretty good tongue-lashing about something that I can't remember (I was six years old, dammit—what do you expect?). I walked over and loudly plopped into a chair.

Ed Jr. peered over the top of his paper and said, "What in the hell is wrong with you boy? You look a little thin in the skin."

"Dad," I stammered, "Mrs. Bennett asked us to say a poem in front of the class today."

"A poem? Damn, that must have been fun. Did you say one, boy?" he queried.

"I did say one, Daddy. Said one that you taught me," I responded.

"One that I taught you? I didn't know that I had taught you any poems."

"Sure you did, Dad. Remember the one you taught me in the garden—listen, listen, the cat is pissin'?"

"You didn't say that in front of the class, did you?" Ed Jr. asked.

"Sure, Dad. I even told Mrs. Bennett that you taught it to me."

"Damn boy, you can't say a poem like that in front of your teacher! That's not a school poem, that's a between-you-and-me poem."

"What's a between-you-and-me poem?" I naively asked.

"Son, sometimes there are things that men say only around other men. Man things. Male things."

"Like what, Dad?"

"Well, boy, things like trucks and women and in-laws and . . . well, hell, you're too young to understand this just yet. You will when you're older. For now, let's just leave it at this—when I tell you that we're discussing man things, they are not to be discussed with anyone else. And that includes your mother."

"Why can't I tell Mama?" I asked.

"Son, I can damn well see that I'd better keep my mouth shut. There are just some things that you don't talk about around women."

"Why?"

"Cause, dammit to hell, I said so. Let's just leave it at that for now. You will understand it better when you're older."

I could accept that answer, plus Ed Jr. appeared to be getting a little red in the face. Best to back off and not pursue this issue any further.

Ed Jr. calmed down a little and sat back in his chair. He grabbed his glass of tea and took a big swallow out of it. As he began to read his newspaper again, I told him that I had a note that Mrs. Bennett had sent to him.

He looked up from his paper and took the envelope from me. As he opened it he asked what the note was about. I told him that I didn't know, but that Mrs. Bennett had given it to me right after I said my poem in front of the class.

"Bet that ruffled her damn feathers," Ed Jr. laughed. That laugh was cut short when he read her note. I can't remember the exact wording of it but it basically said these things: "Your son said a nasty poem in class. He said you taught it to him. If you did teach it to him, you should be very ashamed of yourself. What sort of a parent are you? I expect a response from you."

You could see Ed Jr.'s face get red and the blood vessels in his neck stand up. He was so mad, the explosion that ensued was memorable. "Damned haughty old bitch! Who in the hell does she think she is? All you did was say a little ol' rhyme that all country boys tell. Well, I'll give her a damn response she won't forget!"

With that, Ed Jr. walked over to our phone and picked up the directory. After looking at it a few seconds, he dialed a number. You could hear the phone ring through the earpiece and then a female voice came on and said hello.

"Hello, is this Mrs. Bennett?" Ed Jr. intoned, his face still redder than a whore's knuckles.

I could hear a familiar female voice say, "Yes, it is."

"Well, my name is Ed Williams, Jr. My son is in your class and brought a note home with him today."

"Mr. Williams, you need to be aware of the type poem that Edward said in class today."

"Mrs. Bennett, I know he shouldn't have said that poem but I have one question," Ed Jr. said.

"Certainly, Mr. Williams. Please ask it," Mrs. Bennett responded.

"What country do we live in?" Ed Jr. asked, with a serious expression on his face.

"Of course, we live in America, Mr. Williams," Mrs. Bennett replied.

"Well, let me say first that I'm a Korean War veteran. I proudly served when called on by my country. And one of the things that I risked my ass for over there in those Korean jungles was something called freedom of speech."

"Mr. Williams, I appreciate your service to America, and I do understand what freedom of speech is, but I don't understand what the point is that you're trying to make here," Mrs. Bennett said.

"I'll tell you what the damned point is. On a scale of one to ten, the word *pissin'* is at best a two- or three-point cuss word. I can think of dozens of words that are a lot worse. I've used a few of 'em, too. You're mad at my boy' cause he exercised his right to freedom of speech and used a two-or three-point cuss word. Isn't that so, Mrs. Bennett?" Ed Jr. asked.

I think Mrs. Bennett was somewhat taken aback by this logic. She stammered around a little and said, "Mr. Williams, you're condoning the use of this kind of language?"

"Mrs. Bennett, I'm not raisin' a tea-sipper here," he replied. With that, they both said they understood each other and told each other goodbye.

Ed Jr. turned around, looked at me, and said that I had done nothing wrong and, "If the old biddy gives you any more trouble, just let me know and we'll take another yard out of her ass."

I didn't know what he meant by that, but it sounded good to me. I went on about my business and gained a little more respect for a man who stood up for his convictions to anyone—including my first-grade school teacher.

As I said earlier, this was just the first of many experiences involving poetry with Ed Jr. I found as the years went by that he used it to express himself in many different ways and to make many different points. It had lots of practical applications.

There was the time, for example, when I was around thirteen that my brother Ernest was having some "regularity" problems. What would happen was that he would be pushed for time in the morning, not go to the bathroom, and then wouldn't go at school during the day 'cause, "You never know whose ass has been on those toilets." By the time evening had rolled around he would be in terrible pain. Ed Jr. noticed this situation and lectured us both on the importance of regular bowel habits. He said that it was a poor man who couldn't sleep, eat, or shit, and that one of us should shoot him if he was ever not able to do any of those things.

Ed Jr. figured that reminders would be an appropriate way to get Brother to stop holding back his daily burden. One morning, as we got up to go to school and stumbled sleepily into the kitchen, we noticed a piece of notebook paper on the breakfast table. This simple verse was inscribed:

Two young lads
Off to school
Don't forget to use the stool.
—Fav

("Fav" was Ed Jr.'s pet name for himself. He called my mother "Little Mountain Muv.")

What Ed Jr. was telling us was that we should take a dump before going to school (stool = toilet). Ernest started laughing like hell when he read it, but it had the desired effect. He went to the can, did his duty, and then left with me to catch the school bus. After that there were no more problems.

So, what we can see is that Ed Jr.'s poetry addressed topics not typically addressed by your average, run-of-the-mill poet. He was out there on the cutting edge, plowing fertile ground with each effort. In fact, as I ponder all the poems he has put out over the years, the best thing to do might be to categorize some of them and let you see the inspirations for my current literary efforts.

DINNER BLESSINGS

Corn bread's tough,
Biscuit bread's rough,
Thank God we've got enough.

I'm hungry,
We have a lot,
Let's eat the damn food,
While it's nice and hot.

(My mother gave him hell about this one. He said it one time when we fed the preacher and his wife. Ed Jr. responded that it must not have been too bad as the preacher and his wife ate our food like Indonesian horses).

PSEUDO MOTHER GOOSE

Mary had a little lamb,
She tied him to the heater,
And every time he turned around,
He burned his little peter.

Bathroom Graffiti Poetry

A man's ambition must be mighty small,
To write his name on a shithouse wall.

———————

Oh woe is the man,
With a hole in his pocket,
You might grab some change,
Or your pink trouser rocket!

The Eclectic

A fizzle,
A fazzle,
Don't razzle,
My dazzle.

———————

A fartin' mule's the mule to plow,
A fartin' man's the man to hire.

———————

On again,
Off again,
Gone again,
Finnigan.

Sex

When your pinkie is hard,
But your wife is mad,
Life as you know it,
Is pretty damn sad.

———————

Maw loved Paw,
But Paw loved women,
Maw caught Paw with two in swimmin'.
Here lies Paw.

Old Mother Hubbard,
Sat in her cupboard,
And gave her poor doggie a bone.
And when she bent over,
Ol' Rover, he drove her,
'Cause Rover had a bone of his own.

See, y'all can laugh at these rhymes, but they taught me a couple of things. First off, I did get an early appreciation of matters literary. After hearing these poems it was a natural extension for me to desire reading new ones. So these early efforts of Ed Jr. actually showed me that I liked rhymes and spurred a further interest in reading. They did the trick. I now love to read and have spent many happy hours enjoying a good book or magazine article.

Then, the need to read sort of begat the need to write. I'm still not exactly sure what spurred my desire to write the first book. I've guessed at everything from middle-aged craziness to some sort of impending sense of my demise that would cause me to want to record various aspects of my life. I did find out that Miss Lily, my grandmother and Ed Jr.'s mom, recorded various family events throughout her life by writing them down on scraps of paper. Maybe there is some deep-seated genetic literary trait that I have that didn't manifest itself till I got older. I guess I'll never be real sure about what stirred me to write, but whatever caused it, I'm glad it did. Writing has opened many doors for me and exposed a side of life that I never thought I would become acquainted with. Me interested in the arts or literature—that thought would have been incomprehensible even a few years ago. Whatever the cause, I can clearly tell you from here on out what my motivations for writing are—I enjoy doing it, plus, the publisher gives me lots of money for the effort. So, we're now clear as to my motives on any future literary endeavors I may undertake.

When you sum it all up, I guess it's easy to say that you never really know what particular type of inspiration will drive a young man to go in a certain direction in life. Different people are inspired by different things. For me, the beginning stirrings of my future literary efforts were caused by a few simple, rhyming words detailing a cat is performing a necessary biological act. Only in America, and with a dad like Ed Jr., right?

Chapter 5

ED SR.

❰

His ass was wilder
than yours and mine put together.
— Ed Jr.

Sometimes people ask me about the characters in my books. They'll want to know if they were real, were they really like I've depicted them, did I exaggerate them a lot, etc. It's almost like they want to believe they are real, but find themselves doubting (in various degrees) that they are.

Well, they are real. They're very real and the way—I depicted them is how I saw them. Doesn't mean it's how they were—it's just how I saw them. Honestly, to know how they really are, you'd have to talk to them yourselves. And some of them would probably talk to you, and some of them would look at you like you were crazier than hell. These people are country people—honest and decent, with faults and foibles just like you and me. But I sure loved 'em all—I even reread some of my own stories sometimes, just to make them live again in my mind and heart.

Many people have asked me questions or made comments about Ed Jr. Some want to know if he really did all those things I talk about in my stories. He did. Some tell me that he seems to be a character and that it must have been great to have lived in the same house with him. It was—my brother and I had more fun with him than we could have possibly have had doing tons of other things. He was genuine and real, and we knew down deep that he cared a lot about us.

To this day, I greatly respect people who are straightforward and talk from the heart because of Ed Jr. There's nothing wrong with being yourself, and, if others don't like what you are, well, this is America and they can go hang around with other people. I don't need many people close to my heart as long as I have my family and the Brotherhood. With that emotional anchor in place, I can pretty well face each day as it comes.

All these escapades with Ed Jr. couldn't have happened had it not been for one man—Ed Sr. Y'all can laugh at the things I did, or the things my dad did, but Ed Sr. truly blazed the trail. I've never met a more original man in my life—he was very straightforward and had a great sense of humor. I guess if y'all want some insight as to how Ed Jr. came to be what he is, and how I came to be what I am, then you need to know a little more about Ed Sr.

Ed Sr. was born in 1906 in Monroe County. He grew up in a manner typical of most boys of his era—he had lots of chores to do, he worked hard, and there were little expectations or needs for much formal education. He got through life in a very basic way—it's as simple as that.

As a young man in the twenties and thirties, Ed Sr. was smart enough to buy land when it could be had very cheaply. He bought acreage off what came to be Highway 87 for twenty-five to fifty cents an acre. The reason he did this was that he figured stocks and bonds would go up or down in value, but land always held some worth. He figured if nothing else he could put a house on it and draw from nature the resources that he needed to live.

Ed Sr. married my grandmother Lillian (Miss Lily, and I loved her dearly) in 1928. Ed Jr. was born in 1930, followed by Franklin ("Jew"), Jimmy ("Dog"), Jerry ("Calhoun"), Robert ("Lil' Brother" and "Miss Clawdy"), and the only girl, Lorena. It was a rather large family and they lived simple, productive lives. Ed Sr. and Miss Lily made their living for over forty years by running a general store in downtown Juliette, the one that ended up being the Whistle Stop Café in the movie *Fried Green Tomatoes*.

When I was a small boy, especially in the summertime, going to Ed Sr.'s store was the social and gastronomical highlight of my day. If Ed Jr. was home he'd get Brother and me and ride down to the store early in the morning—usually around nine or ten o'clock. He would give each of us a dime to spend on junk. You might think that that was a little cheap, but in Juliette during the 1960s, a dime would buy you a Coke and candy bar. We each felt like that dime was a million bucks when we strolled into Ed Sr.'s store.

There were some unique characters who hung around the front of Ed Sr.'s store and whom I got to know over the years. There was Wig, an old black man who was best known for loving brownies. As the story went, he could eat a whole plate of them at one sitting. Ed Sr. got a little tired of Wig hanging around all the time, but didn't quite know how to get him to leave. After pondering his dilemma, Ed Sr. got Miss Lily to mix up a batch of brownies up for him on the pretext of giving them as a present. While Miss Lily's attention was diverted, Ed Sr. dropped a fairly massive amount of Ex-Lax (the chocolate kind) into the brownie mix. Miss Lily didn't notice, and stirred it right into the soft brownie mixture. After a couple of hours, Ed Sr. had a plate full of doctored brownies to take to his good friend, Wig.

Wig was waiting on the store's porch for Ed Sr. when he strolled up with his brownies. He then launched into a cock-and-bull story about how much he valued Wig's friendship, talked about how close they'd become, and then presented the brownies. Wig was so touched that he killed the plate without even pausing to drink anything. Ed Sr. said that it took a lot of strength not to laugh out loud, but he had an important point to make.

Wig sat around for about forty-five minutes after he ate those brownies. After that, according to eyewitness accounts, Wig began looking a bit thin in the skin. After another ten minutes or so, Wig vaulted up from the store bench, ran across the railroad tracks, and sprinted quickly into the woods.

An hour passed, and a very pale and weak-looking Wig returned to the store porch. Ed Sr. walked out, and, utilizing a pensive Foskey-type facial expression, quizzed Wig as to what was wrong?

"Mista Ed, I be feelin' good when I gots here dis morning. And I sho' appreciated dem brownies. Only thing was, after I et 'em, my stomach gots to bubblin'. Got to hurting so damn bad that I was afred to stay here. Had to go out in the woods and shit hard," stated Wig.

"And how are you now, Wig?" replied Ed Sr. with that serious expression still goin'.

"Mista Ed, I been sick befo', and I's had the shits befo', but dis is the first time I ever had an atomic asshole! I sho' hope it don't turn sour on me again 'cause I like to have covered dat hill over yonder."

Even Ed Sr. couldn't hold out when Wig said this, and he started laughing like crazy. He also noticed that this experience did cut Wig's store loitering time down a little—at least for a couple of weeks.

Another person I saw on the store frontporch a lot was Edwin Chambers. His nickname happened to be "Hun." Where the "Hun" came from I don't know, but that's what Ed Sr. always called him.

One of Hun's most noticeable attributes was that he was extremely well-endowed from a genitalia standpoint. He was also a very simple man, as his IQ was somewhere in the neighborhood of Forrest Gump's. Ed Sr. noticed Hun's large trouser python one summer day after accidentally spotting him taking a leak out behind his store. He made the following gentle observation to Ed Jr. as we were visiting the store the morning after his discovery.

"Damned if I didn't see something yesterday morning that surprised me," Ed Sr. stated.

"What was that, ol' man?" Ed Jr. replied.

"Ole Hun was out back takin' a piss yesterday morning. If you painted spots on his dick, you'd swear it was a damned giraffe's neck. Biggest damn cock I ever saw—tragedy is, he wouldn't know what to do with it if he had to," opined Ed Sr.

"I can't believe you'd notice his root monkey! Are you sure you're feeling okay, old man?" Ed Jr. asked.

"The day I wouldn't notice a tree stump cock like that is the day I'll use piss for salad dressing," replied Ed Sr.

This pretty much ended this tender exchange of words. Needless to say, the dialogues between Ed Sr. and Ed Jr. from over the years were not exactly boilerplate examples for the prim and proper of this world. They took the word *basic* and gave it a rich, new meaning.

As I got older, episodes like these confirmed to me that Ed Sr. was a stark individualist. He did unusual things like having a free-standing office built about one hundred feet off his master bedroom. He would escape there when people he didn't want to see came by to visit him (like most of Miss Lily's relatives). I loved going there (and was honored that he allowed me inside) because he had all sorts of interesting memorabilia tacked up on the walls—stuff like baseball headlines from newspapers, pictures of semi-naked women, and a large pink plastic ass that made a Bronx cheer when you touched one of the cheeks. He loved baseball and could cuss the Braves ten times better than even Ed Jr. could. He visited New York one time and saw the Yankees play at Yankee Stadium. A complete telegraph set was in place on his desk—he had gotten it from his years of employment as a telegraph operator for the railroad. He loved a good, dirty joke and enjoyed being around people he was comfortable with. I loved hearing him tell stories 'cause no one was better at spinning a yarn than he was. I can remember laughing till my stomach knotted up at some of the things he'd say to me.

When I got old enough to date, Ed Sr. took me aside and gave me the first real piece of relationship information I had ever gotten. I was sixteen, and just beginning to date a little. Of course, being the sensitive type he is, Ed Jr. kindly let Ed Sr. know this one day when we visited his store. I was looking around the candy counter when I heard Ed Jr. say, "Well, there's another Ed Williams about to be turned loose on these young gals around here." Course, Eds Sr. and Jr. laughed like hell about the statement, and, when their laughter subsided, Ed Sr. said, "Come on over here, boy."

Being the obedient grandson that I was, I walked quickly over to where Ed Sr. and my dad were standing. Ed Sr. smiled, looked at me, and said, "Boy, I hear you're startin' to see the wimmen."

"Yes sir," I humbly replied.

"Boy, have you honed the tulip yet?" Ed Sr. asked.

"I've just started dating, sir," I replied, not sure as to whether or not I should honestly answer his question.

"Boy, there's no need to beat around the bush when it comes to tulip honing. Did I ever tell you about the first time I screwed a woman?" he asked.

"No sir, I can't say that you have," I cleverly replied.

"Well, there was this little ol' Dorsett gal that lived down the way from us when I was growing up. Ever time I'd walk by, she'd smile at me and look. You know what that means, boy?" the senior Ed queried.

"What?"

"It means that she wanted more from me than just a smile. Now, I knew what I had to do."

He went on to say that one afternoon he had told this Dorsett girl that he was coming by to see her that evening. He did so, and ended up sitting on her front porch swing, swaying back and forth. He said that they smiled at each other a lot and exchanged cat glances.

As the evening progressed, things got a little more interesting. "We smiled at each other like we'd been in the briars. Then, I kissed her right on the lips—she liked it too, although you could tell that she hadn't been kissed a lot. I figured she needed practice, so I kept on kissin' her."

"Didn't take much of that and my cock was harder than a British pencil. After a few more minutes, I pulled away from her and looked her dead in her eyes. Then, before she could say anything, I raised both fists up like a boxer would."

"Why in the world would you raise both fists?" I naively inquired.

"Because boy, you have to be direct," Ed Sr. said.

I figured at this point that he was gonna shock me and say that he punched out the Dorsett girl or something. Rather than do that, Ed Sr. told her the following, "I've come to fuck or fight."

I couldn't believe what Ed Sr. said. Even Ed Jr. got real quiet. As the hearing returned to my ears, I heard Ed Sr. say that the Dorsett girl yelled, "What?"

He replied, looking right in her face, "I've walked down the road to see you here at night. It's hot, and I've got on nice clothes. I smell good, too, and I ain't here to play games. What will it be?"

The Dorsett girl stammered again, "You've got to be kidding."

Ed Sr. got his face close to hers and whispered, "Try me."

I was dying to know what the Dorsett girl's answer was. I looked directly at Ed Sr. and said, "God, tell me how she answered!"

Ed Sr. propped up over on the countertop, leaned over, and said, "I didn't go home with any bruises on me, boy."

I laughed like hell, thought he was full of bull, and told him so. He laughed real hard at this and said that he liked the fact I had some spunk about me. But facts were facts—he had actually gotten laid using this technique. And he talked more with me about it until he was convinced I believed him.

After all that, I told him I thought I might try a little bit different approach to the art of pitching woo. He told me that was okay, but "your bone is gonna stay dry." At this, he and Ed Jr. laughed, and the conversation switched to more important things, like how the New York Yankees were doing or something.

After that, I sought out my grandfather deliberately, enjoying the hell out of his stories and opinions. We would talk about so many different things—I almost think Ed Sr. took these times to sort of imbue me with his philosophies. It was like there was this unspoken thing, that the elder Eds sort of nurtured the younger ones to insure that they had the proper value systems installed. Plus, there was just so much creativity and wildness about my dad and grandfather that it was great fun merely having conversations with them.

It was not only the subject of lovemaking that Ed Sr. gave me valuable guidance on. Believe it or not, I learned about the true meaning of Christmas and Santa Claus from him. I can still hear his words at the old store on a fall afternoon long ago.

"Boy, we're gettin' powerful close to Christmas, ain't we?"

"Yeah, Granddaddy, we are," I astutely replied.

"Gotta remember one thing, boy."

"What's that?" I replied.

"Santa Claus will screw you blind if you don't watch him."

"What?"

"Santa Claus will screw you blind if you let him."

I honestly thought that Ed Sr. must have been drinking or something. I asked him again to repeat what he had just said.

"Santa Claus would steal the pennies off a dead man."

He was just so damn matter of fact about it. It didn't take a genius to see that Ed Sr. had suffered a less than positive experience with Santa Claus. I asked him why he felt so poorly towards him.

"Because he's a cheap, money-grubbing old bastard—that's why," he resolutely explained.

I was amazed beyond words at this point. I had a sort of perverted sense of awe towards a man who would malign Santa himself. I didn't have to wait for an explanation of these feelings, though, as Ed Sr. launched right into his story.

"When I was about twelve years old I wanted a damn wagon for Christmas. A nice red one with big wheels on it. Most of the kids that lived around us had at least one wagon. We didn't have shit. Anyway, I thought and thought about that wagon."

"My mama told me that I should write a letter to Santa and tell him what I wanted. Now, you have to remember that 'cause we lived so far out in the country you could be fifteen or sixteen before you found out the truth about Santa Claus. Anyway, I scrounged around one evening and found some paper. Then, I sat down one night in front of a kerosene lamp and wrote the damn thing. It hurt my eyes 'cause the light was so bad and the damn letter took over an hour to write. I kept askin' Mama how to spell certain words—I didn't want to ask Daddy 'cause he would thought I was a pansy for writin' a letter to Santa anyway. After awhile, I finished the damn thing and gave it to my mother to send off."

I started smilin' and propped up, 'cause I could tell this was gonna be a good story. I deliberately gave my grandfather one of my best innocent facial expressions, and urged him to tell more.

"In those days, winters were hell. You had to get heat from an ol' wood stove. Frank (his brother, my great-uncle) and I went in and out of our house a hundred times each day fetchin' wood to keep that hot bastard stocked up. One mornin', we were outside getting wood and talking 'bout Christmas."

"I sure wish I'd get a damn wagon this year," said Ed Sr.

"Not a prayer," replied Frank, "that bastard Santa didn't even bring me a bolo paddle (remember the paddles that had a long rubber band on them and a ball attached at the end?) last year. You know, he ought to have to pay for all the damn misery he spreads around. Why, Smith Hammond up the street got a bicycle last Christmas."

"Well," said Ed Sr., "Smith is such a kiss-ass that it's no wonder. You know, regular guys like us aren't gonna get a break from a guy like Santa. He only caters to mama's boys and daffodils like Smith."

Frank grumbled, "What makes it all the worse is that he expects you to kiss his ass for some raisins and nuts—that's all the fat shit left me last year."

"No damn worse than the oranges and walnuts that I got," replied Ed Sr.

"You know," Frank added, "why do we care if we're good or not? Doesn't matter, it seems to me. You can be good all year and all you get for it is raisins and nuts."

"I'd like to kick Santa's damn nuts," exclaimed Ed Sr. "You know something, Frank?"

"What?"

"Santa ought to have to pay for all the damn misery he's given us," Ed Sr. stated, in his usual no-bullshit delivery.

"How can you make Santa pay?"

"Well, I think I have an idea," Ed Sr. replied, and the two boys then began devising a plan.

The following days and nights passed rather quickly, as the two young boys devised their plan of revenge against Santa. They discussed it over and over. Modified it once or twice to get it just right. They felt guilty at times—devising a plan to punish Santa Claus. But it had to be done—after all, right was right. Santa had to learn that he couldn't just shit all over people, especially two young boys who expected more than walnuts and raisins for Christmas. He hadn't treated them fairly so he had to pay. It was as simple as that.

Christmas Eve finally rolled around and my great-grandmother must have noticed the more-than-usual tension on the faces of her two young sons. As they were getting ready for bed, Ed Sr. told me that she had asked both Frank and he if they had fevers or something. It was very obvious to her that both boys were very fidgety that night.

She couldn't have known that they intended to sit up all evening and wait on Santa. And not to welcome him either—in Ed Sr.'s words, "we were gonna whip Santa's ass."

That was the plan they'd hatched—sit up, wait, and attack Santa when he entered the living room later on in the evening. I was amazed when Ed Sr. told me this. The whole thing was surreal. I mean, think about it—whipping Santa's ass? Attacking Santa? Sounded like a plot out of a bad grade B horror flick. At this point, though, I knew he was serious. I could tell by his expression and his tone of voice. And I wanted him to keep on talking—I had to know exactly what he and Frank had done to Santa.

Didn't take long to find out, either. Ed Sr. cleared his throat and continued this heart-wrenching tale. "Mama finally made Frank and me go to bed. We both tried to look relaxed, but when a man is about to go to war it's damn hard to relax. We didn't want to just kick Santa's ass. We wanted to embarrass him and let him know that kids want toys—not oranges and socks and crap. Santa was gettin' sorta arrogant in our opinion. We felt like the old fart thought that all he had to do was bring us anything and that we'd have to like it. Well, the way Frank and I saw it, it was time for Santa's attitude to change."

Frank and Ed Sr. decided to sleep in shifts, so that one would be awake when Santa got there. Ed Sr. took the first shift, and Frank nodded off to sleep momentarily.

What the boys didn't know was there was actually going to be a physical appearance in their house by Santa Claus that evening. It seems that during this era in Juliette there was an established custom whereby one of the neighborhood men dressed up as Santa Claus each year and placed presents under each child's tree. If you think about it, it's a very nice, family-oriented, heartwarming Christmas custom.

Well, heartwarming until Ed Sr. added this particular episode to Christmas folklore. It just so happened that on this particular evening my great-grandfather, Ed Sr.'s dad, was playing Santa. I can imagine this good Samaritan having to put on all the Santa get-up, and then having to walk all over the neighborhood distributing Christmas toys. Don't you know that he was sweaty, tired, and whipped out from all his efforts?

By Ed Sr.'s account, Ed One (Edward Masden Williams, shortened to "Ed One" for future reference) arrived back at his own home shortly after midnight. This was due to the fact that whomever played Santa each year was expected to distribute all the other gifts first before distributing his own family's gifts. Anyway, Ed One pulled in very late that night, ready to put his children's gifts under the tree, and then lay down for some well-deserved rest.

When Ed One arrived home, Frank was up as it was his shift to be awake. Frank heard some muffled sounds that seemed to be emanating from the kitchen. After hearing them for a few seconds, he became convinced that Santa had arrived. With trembling hands, he leaned over and shook Ed Sr. awake.

"Ed!" Frank exclaimed. "That stingy bastard is here!"

"Who?" mumbled Ed Sr.

"Santa," replied Frank. He then shook Ed Sr. some more. "We got to get our asses in there before he gets away!"

Ed Sr. and Frank snuck out of their bed and tiptoed down the hall. They walked very quietly and were both scared to death. What if Santa saw them, got pissed, and didn't leave them anything? What if they were struck blind or something? Santa did have a quasi-religious connotation to these boys. You can imagine them being very concerned over just what problems their plan might lead to.

The two boys stopped at the edge of the living room. Then, they squatted down low and peeped around the edge of the door.

They gasped at what they saw. Strolling resolutely into the room was Santa Claus himself. There was no mistaking it—the red suit, the white beard, his large red toy sack, etc. It definitely was the real Santa!

Ed Sr. said that he then saw Santa reach inside his bag and pull out a box of raisins. He took this box and placed it inside Frank's stocking. According to Ed Sr., Frank was livid.

"That cheap sonofabitch!" Frank muttered. "Wait on him all year just to get some raisins. This is it!"

Ed Sr. said that at this point Santa's ass had to be whupped. The only thing left to be decided was exactly how to subdue him. He looked at Frank and said,

"I'll hit him high and you aim for his knees."

They were gonna high-low Santa! I was laughing so hard at the thought that Ed Sr. gave me a bemused, yet stern, look. I quickly composed myself so that he wouldn't get sidetracked off this unusual story.

One can only imagine Ed One's surprise to see his two large sons running straight across the room towards him. Ed Sr. said that they ran real fast and knocked the hell out of Santa upon impact. He said that he slammed into Santa's chest just as Frank smashed into Santa's knees. Ed Sr. said it was a damn good tackle, and that he could feel Santa's body give.

Ed One was knocked right into the Christmas tree! The tree's decorations, limbs, and tinsel flew everywhere. In fact, the impact split the tree into three large pieces. Gifts were smashed or sent flying across the room. Ed Sr. likened the whole thing to a major bomb explosion.

The myth of Santa died very quickly for these two boys. The force of the tackle knocked off Ed One's beard and disguise. Then, "Santa" was heard saying some things that were not very Santa-like. Stuff like, "You two big, stupid shits! What in the hell do y'all think you're doing? I swear to God y'all have broken my damn leg!" quoteth Ed One.

"Dad? Damn, we didn't realize it was you!" said Frank.

"You don't mean you've been Santa the whole time?" asked Ed Sr. When Ed One nodded that he had, Ed Sr. was even more incensed.

"You mean to tell me that all this Santa shit has been an act? That I've been gooder than hell all year, year after year, just so that you can give me some damn raisins? What a gyp—why didn't you tell us the truth earlier?" Ed Sr. steamed.

"You two boys are crazier than hell. What kids attack Santa? You two big lummoxes ought to be ashamed of what you just did!" replied Ed One.

"Wait a damn minute," said Ed Sr., "You lied to us, dressed up in a disguise to trick us, and then you screw us on the gifts? And you're mad? Hell, we're the ones who have a right to be mad!"

Ed One thought this one over, and gave Ed Sr. a pensive, Foskey-type expression,

"You know son, you may be right. I don't like it that y'all just tackled my ass but I do have to admit this is a pretty rotten scam that we pull on you kids each year. Tell you what—let's drop this Santa shit, and from here on out we'll just exchange gifts with each other."

"Dad, that's fine but the damn problem is all you give us is raisins and nuts and shit like that for Christmas each year," emphasized Frank.

"You know, I guess you're right, Frank. Raisins and nuts ain't much to look forward to. I guess now I can understand why you wanted to whip Santa's ass," replied Ed One.

Ed Sr. went on to tell me that after this Christmas the following ones were much better. They didn't have to go through the Santa charade, and both he and Frank got much better gifts than they had received in the past.

As he finished this story, Ed Sr. laughed as he remembered how his mom had fervently prayed to God for several weeks afterwards, begging him not to send her two Santa-tackling boys straight to hell. When a few weeks passed and God had not wreaked some sort of evil vengeance on them, she felt much better and slowly forgot about this tender episode.

As Ed Sr. wound down with his story, I was both laughing and mildly awed by the whole thing. He was so direct and matter-of-fact about attacking Santa. He was also convinced that he and Frank had done the right thing. I asked him why he didn't feel really funny about mauling Santa. Ed Sr. replied that right was right and that Santa had it coming to him. For Ed Sr., the rules of life applied equally, whether you were Santa or Wig. Made no difference. In Ed Sr.'s eyes, Santa had screwed up and had to pay the price. And from the sound of it, Santa paid it in full.

I always think about this story each year around Christmas time. To tell you the truth, the memory of it comes in handy when you are endur-ing some particularly saccharine sweet Christmas event. I can just envision Ed Sr. and Frank high-lowing Santa as they tackled him. You have to smile or laugh at the mere thought. I also found in future years that this story always got tons of laughs from those I told it to. It is just so different—yet all it was, was Ed Sr. being true to himself. That's how he conducted his life—whatever he was, he was honest with himself. A trait more people should have, for sure.

Being true to himself also meant telling a person if they were too ugly to be seen out in public. Ed Sr. did this one time—he actually told someone to his face that he was too ugly to be out walking in public. The recipient of this tender message was one Charlie Pound.

Legend around Juliette has it that Charlie Pound could make an elephant's eyes hurt because he was so ugly. Ed Jr. described him as a "badger with human eyes and lips." Needless to say, Charlie was more than a bit beaten with the proverbial ugly stick. Ed Jr. even said that Charlie's eyes and ears were ugly. Suffice it to say, Charlie Pound was not going to be winning any beauty pageants in the foreseeable future.

As the story goes, Ed Sr. was driving his truck to Forsyth one bright April morning. He took a slow, leisurely drive, and several people were out walking alongside the roads. This was commonplace during this era—drivers often slowed down to a crawl and had conversations with people who happened to be walking alongside the roads. Since travel by foot was very common during this era, there were lots of opportunities for conversations between drivers and walkers.

On this particular morning, Charlie Pound happened to be walking down the road towards Juliette. Ed Sr. was using the same road to leave Juliette and go towards Forsyth. This set the scene for the encounter he and Charlie were about to have.

Ed Sr. told me that as his truck got within a quarter mile of the man walking towards him he could tell it was Charlie Pound. When I asked him how he could know this if he was a quarter mile away, he replied, "Ugly carries, boy." He then went on to explain that an ugly person can be seen from farther off than a good-looking person. This is because the ugly person makes our eyes focus harder. Ed Sr. said it was a scientific fact that our eyes can't comprehend how ugly the person is, and they work harder to be sure that what they are seeing is reality . My grandfather added that the eyes do this to be sure that the mind isn't playing a trick on them about the excessive ugliness being viewed.

I could see the logic in this. Made sense to me, in a convoluted sort of way. Ed Sr. gave me a knowing smile when he saw that his words were being understood and agreed with. He then continued on with his story.

"I kept drivin', boy, and sure enough, I was right. It was Charlie Pound. He was wearing those same damn old overalls he wore all the time and a white t-shirt. Had a big chaw of tobacco goin' too, which made his damn face look that much more ugly. Imagine, boy, a six-foot badger comin' towards you with a chaw of tobacco in his mouth. Can't get much uglier than that, can you?"

I had to agree with him on that point.

"I drove my truck up close to Charlie," Ed Sr. continued. "He walked right up to me and stuck his damn head in the window. Ugly from a good distance off is one thing, but havin' to see it up close? He looked like someone had used his head for battin' practice! He started talkin', and you could see that brown chewin' tobacco goin' in his mouth. Anyway you looked at it, he was ugly and then some."

I busted out laughing.

"Charlie started talkin' to me 'bout some damn mules he owned that had dysentery. Told me how he couldn't use 'em for a damn thing, they were so sick. I just couldn't take it anymore—that ugly head so close to me, the tobacco, his breath smelling like rancid ham. I said to hell with it, looked him right in the eye and said, 'Charlie, you are too damn ugly.'

"He looked sorta surprised and stared at me. Then, I guess he thought he hadn't heard me right, so he kept right on talkin'.

"I looked him right in the eye again and yelled, 'Charlie you are TOO DAMN UGLY!' He stopped talkin'. Figured I'd better go ahead and just say my piece. I looked him in the eye and told him, 'Charlie, you're a damn good man but you are also an ugly sonofabitch. Now, I know that you can't help being ugly—God dealt you that poor hand. But you can damn well control what you do! Charlie, the rest of us shouldn't have to look at your ugly ass in broad daylight. You should go home and only get out in the late afternoon or evening, when you can't be seen as easily. I say this only for your own good.' "

Ed Sr. said Charlie thanked him for his insights and headed on down the road. He also said that Charlie didn't seem to venture out much in the daytime after that.

I gave Ed Sr. static about being so blunt with the guy. When I did, he looked at me as if he couldn't believe I had descended from his loins. He reminded me that people get sick and vomit, but you don't want to watch them doing it. He then said he would just as soon have watched someone vomit as to have to look at Charlie. Pausing to collect his thoughts, he then said something to me that I'll remember for the rest of my life.

"Being honest may hurt people sometimes, but being less than honest hurts them all the time."

How can you rebut that? I then realized that underneath all these funny stories was a very wise and decent man. A man who didn't have a whole lot of use for phoniness and hypocrisy. A man who could look at himself in a mirror each day and not feel too much shame about what he was or what he had done.

Ed Sr. lived until he was seventy-seven years old. Almost till the last he was very vibrant and alive. He cussed the Braves on a daily basis and typed some Morse code out on his telegraph set from time to time. He still ran the old store and chatted with everyone who came by about anything they wanted to talk about. Wig kept coming to the old store each day until the day he died. I can remember going to Wig's funeral and noticing Ed Sr. there. Ed Sr. didn't attend too many functions, but he did pay his last respects to the little black man who had spent so many hours sitting on the front porch of his store. When the preacher was talking about Wig I remember seeing Ed Sr.'s face grow taut, and I could tell he was fighting back tears. It moved me to see the loyalty and friendship that he was feeling towards his departed friend.

In my lifetime, I have been fortunate enough to have done some good things. I have received some awards and have done reasonably well in business and sports. I am fortunate to have a good wife and two excellent children. God blessed me as well by allowing me to be in the Brotherhood. But out of all these things, one statement that was spoken to me by Ed Sr. had more meaning than anything else any other person has ever said.

He said it one Saturday morning when I was seventeen years old. Ed Jr. had run me down to the store that day because I had scored a touchdown against Telfair County the night before.

Ed Jr. related my achievement with pride to Ed Sr. He also talked about how well I was doing in school and how some of the girls liked me and stuff. I was sorta embarrassed by it all, but Ed Jr. said it in a very sincere manner. Ed Sr. listened closely and then looked at me. He slowly walked over to where I was standing, put his hand on my shoulder, and said, "I'm proud you have my name."

I looked at him and saw how serious he was. I had to swallow really hard to keep from getting choked up. Ed Sr. was not a man given to sentimentality, but here he was, basically telling me that he loved me and was proud I bore his name. That approval meant so much to me then and means even more to me today.

When they buried Ed Sr. back in 1981, I remembered him saying those words to me. I am remembering them again as I write these lines. I sure hope that somewhere out there, he can see that I haven't forgotten, and that I am very proud to have gone through life carrying his name.

Chapter 6
THE SANCTITY
OF THE SUPER BOWL

☾

I froze my ass off in those Korean rice paddies for the
chance to watch this.
—Ed Jr.

I know I told y'all about Ed Jr.'s love of sports in my first epistle, *Sex,*
Dead Dogs, and Me. His passion for sports transcends just about
any other interests he has in life. There's just something about competition and athletics that has a visceral appeal to him. Ed Jr., without question, is one of the most competitive individuals I have ever known.

We always watched the major sports together—football, baseball,
and basketball. Football was his unquestioned favorite of them all.
When Brother and I played football at Mary Persons High, Ed Jr.
attended all the games. This was true even if he had to swap shifts at the
gas plant (he worked for almost forty years at Southern Natural Gas
Company), or make any other sorts of sacrifices to see the games. He
didn't miss them for any reason.

This love of football spilled over into Sunday afternoons at our
house. Typically, on Sundays my mom would leave and go visit friends.
She had to do this because Ed Jr., Brother, and I commandeered the den
to watch pro football. We always took in the Falcons' games, no matter
how dismal they were. Back then, the Falcons didn't win—come to
think of it, they didn't win until one time back in '98 when Coach
Reeves took the team to the Super Bowl. Even so, we faithfully watched
them each weekend, hoping for a miracle and the resultant win to occur.

Ed Jr. had (and still has) definitive opinions about some of the past
Falcons' players. He especially disliked Steve Bartkowski. Now for those
of you who don't know Steve Bartkowski, he was probably the best over-

all quarterback the Falcons ever had. The difficulty was that early on in his career, he took a beating on account of the poor play of the Falcons' offensive line. I can remember him taking sack after merciless sack. Sometimes, I think the beating he took in his early years caused him later on to hurry throws, which ultimately ended up as either bad throws or costly interceptions.

Ed Jr. didn't give a damn about all this. He basically thought Bartkowski was gutless and less than a man for not taking the hits. He didn't hide his feelings either, as the following direct quotes would indicate:

(After Bartkowski threw a record number of interceptions in a game), "If I was the coach of the Falcons, I wouldn't even let the sorry bastard go home with the rest of the team. I'd put him on a Greyhound and tell the driver not to be in a hurry!"

"If brains were shit, Bartkowski couldn't make a bean fart."

(One of my favorites, the "ass" trilogy): "I can't understand how the Falcons can watch him and not feel the need to put a shoe in his ass!"

And, "You can't even tell me that some of the players don't want to kick his ass!"

And the ever-popular, "I'd hate to have worked like hell all afternoon just to watch his gutless ass throw the whole ballgame away!"

When Bartkowski retired from football, Ed Jr. was extremely happy. He felt that this would be all the impetus the Falcons would need to become a winning team. As the following ten to fifteen years showed, it didn't prove to be the case. If anything, the Falcons have regressed instead of improved, except for the Super Bowl year. All those bleak years did not improve Ed Jr.'s demeanor any—he cussed and bemoaned the Falcons like crazy, telling people that they made him faithfully lose his religion each Sunday. As of the last few years, his most vehement Falcons' invective was aimed at one Jeff George.

For those of you who don't know Jeff George, he was the quarterback for the Falcons a few years ago. I think he only played for them for two or three years. He ended up his Falcons career by getting suspended and ultimately released for becoming involved in a screamfest with Coach June Jones during one of the Falcons' games. After this episode, the Falcons went on to a glorious 3-13 record—so glorious that June Jones lost his job and George ended up going from team to team to team. The whole story of his tenure with the team was yet another classic example of Falcons mismanagement.

Jeff began his pro career with the Indianapolis Colts. After a few seasons there, he was openly dissatisfied. The Colts feverishly looked for a sucker to unload him upon, and, lo and behold, the Falcons were interested! We gave up several first-round draft picks and God knows what else to get him.

Jeff came to Atlanta and was immediately disliked by Ed Jr. The reason for this is that he saw Jeff George as a modern-day version of Bartkowski. In-his words, "Jeff can throw the ball one hundred yards, but has a dime store head. Why in the hell can't we get a smart quarterback?" This rant got worse a few years ago when the Falcons traded back-up quarterback Bret Favre to the Green Bay Packers. Bret, at this point in time, has been the league MVP twice and the Packers have won the Super Bowl with him as their quarterback. Jeff George, on the other hand, ended up being dealt to the Oakland Raiders, and since then has been traded from team to team to team. Just before signing with Oakland he turned down a 5-year, 30-million-dollar contract to play for the Seattle Seahawks. He said he did this because he wasn't sure he wanted to play football in Seattle. For 30 million dollars I would paint my ass blue and do the Macarena naked at church. I think June Jones ended up becoming an assistant coach for another pro team, and then a college coach.

Despite all the Falcons' problems, we watched their games faithfully each week. All this time spent watching their games whetted our appetites for the ultimate competition in pro football—the playoffs. After a year of Falcons football, the three of us savored the playoffs like a bum savors Ripple. Given how much we loved them, you can begin to imagine what the Super Bowl meant to the three of us.

For Ed Jr., the Super Bowl was the holy grail of all professional sports. The ultimate game—the one for all the marbles. He never missed one, and was incredulous that every living American was not in front of their television sets watching it as well. He liked to watch the game in complete silence, with only my brother and me enjoying it with him.

The most memorable Super Bowl game I can ever remember was the one played in 1968. This was the classic confrontation between the Baltimore Colts and the New York Jets. The Colts were huge favorites, but the brash Jets' quarterback, Joe Namath, flatly predicted that his team would win the game.

Ed Jr. felt like Broadway Joe had lost his mind. He was incredulous that he could even entertain the thought that his team might win. "There's more chance of me dabbin' on perfume than there is of that," he stated with his usual firm conviction.

Super Bowl Sunday of 1968 finally came around. Ed Jr.'s first item of business was to run my mom out of the house for the afternoon. We had to do this 'cause she had this annoying habit of getting on to us for cussing during the game, or for burping, or for any other means of self-expression we chose to indulge in. As he put it, "Barbara, it's the only damn time I can be myself and you don't wanna even let me do that! On Super Bowl Sunday, dammit, we are watching football the way it was intended to be watched." Thus said, my mom went off to visit the neighbors while Ed Jr., Brother, and I watched the game in near perfect solitude.

In 1968, there was not near as much pregame hoopla as there is now. Despite that, we had watched about two hours worth of pre-game stuff when the phone started ringing. Kickoff was only about ten minutes away.

Ed Jr. stomped into the kitchen and answered it. We could hear some low mumbling, and then these words, spoken loudly, "What? You've got to be kidding. Doesn't that idiot know that the damn Super Bowl is on and kickoff is in ten minutes? I can't believe that there's anyone in America that doesn't know this game is on and . . . and . . . what a dumb sonofabitch!"

He slammed down the phone. Brother and I jumped up and ran into the kitchen to find out what was going on.

"That damn Preacher Garrett and his addled-headed wife decided today, out of all days, that he's gonna visit everybody at the church. That was Betty Banks—he just left her house and is on the way up here! If he gets here he'll never stop talking. His old lady will be good for three damn hours!" Strangely enough, after this outburst, the redness in his face faded away and Ed Jr. stopped yelling. He got a pensive, Foskey-type expression going on his face and said, "We've got to have a plan. I'm not giving up on the Super Bowl to listen to ol' lady Garrett talk about the damn corns on her feet! Ernest, cut off every light in the house. Al, close off all the shutters and blinds! I'll cut the sound off on the TV. If we're lucky, the old bastard will think we're not home!"

It was a brilliant plan, but the only problem was that we only had about five minutes in which to execute it. Nonetheless, we ran around like blurs and did our assigned duties. We soon secured the house, squatted in the den in front of our now soundless TV set (to avoid being seen through the windows of our house), and waited to see what was gonna happen.

We heard a car driving slowly up the road to our house. Soon, the crunch of gravel indicated that the car was coming up our driveway. Brother rushed over to the living room window to see who it was, but

Ed Jr. said, "Dammit, they'll see you!" He rushed back in the den, and, in about another minute, the knocks on our door began. You won't believe this, but the Preacher and Mrs. Garrett must have knocked at least twenty times! My dad just grimaced and muttered under his breath about how anyone could be so stupid as to visit someone on Super Bowl Sunday. Finally, after all those knocks, the Garretts gave up and left. (The only other thing I remember about this episode was that Mrs. Garrett smoked a lot and was hacking like hell at the front door. My dad remarked, "Isn't that sweet? Nothing I'd rather do than listen to old lady Garrett croup and wheeze while the Super Bowl is on.")

Ed Jr. stood up from his squatted position, cleared his throat, and made a speech about the fundamental rights of Americans. He then went on to talk about standing up for yourself, and said, "I'm a Korean War veteran, and I'll be damned if I have to give up my right to enjoy the Super Bowl!" The only thing I can guess he meant by this comment was he felt if he was denied the chance to watch the game that one of his inalienable rights as an American was being violated. We then proceeded to watch it—Ed Jr. was astonished at the outcome, in fact, he felt that the mob had paid off some of the Colts' players to throw the game. Nonetheless, we had a good time and did get to watch the entire Super Bowl game in peace. The only other thing I remember about this episode was that next Sunday at church Preacher Garrett remarked to my mom and dad that he was real sorry that he and Mrs. Garrett had not been able to visit with us the previous Sunday. My mother was puzzled by this comment, mentioned it to Ed Jr., but he acted as if he didn't know what she was talking about.

Ed Jr. went on from this to watch every Super Bowl game that has been played since. He has cussed some teams, beamed with pride at some, and marveled at some of the exploits that have occurred. The one thing that was real in '68, and is still very real now, is his passion for competition. That need to win. His desire for victory can best be summed up in the words he uttered right after the Broncos beat our Falcons a few years ago: "A whupped ass is a whupped ass. The Falcons were good, but not good enough. Is anything left in the refrigerator?"

Says it all, don't it?

CHAPTER 7
RASSLIN' AND RISKIN' (OUR ASSES)

☾

I didn't know whether to nut up,
or just forget about the whole thing.
— Hugh

I never knew that attending a pro wrestling match could pose hazards to the health of the spectator. But, twenty-hree years ago, Ray, Hugh, and I found ourselves in a situation where our lives were literally threatened because we exercised our right to free speech at a pro wrestling show. You don't believe me? Then just sit back, relax, and let me chronicle how a simple night of pro wrestling turned into yet another low-keyed Brotherhood adventure.

As mentioned in my first book, we all attended school at Georgia College in Milledgeville, Georgia. We all loved going to school there, but, to be honest, Milledgeville is not exactly what you'd call a hotbed of excitement. Most of us who went to school there spent more than one night not doing much of anything. Well, when you're in the Brotherhood and faced with this situation, you get out and create your own excitement.

One Tuesday in 1976, that's exactly what the three of us did. The entire Brotherhood found itself lounging around in Hugh's dorm room early on this particular afternoon. Hugh had tacked up a picture on his wall of a *Playboy* centerfold, and the three of us were discussing exactly what sorts of perversions we would enjoy inflicting upon her. This conversation sorta languished along when Hugh said, "Damn, I'm tired of just sitting here on my ass. There's gotta be something we can do."

Ray chimed in that one of our friends had just dated a girl who appeared to have the morals of an Arkansas politician. He suggested that we should give her a call to see if one of us could get lucky and snag a date with her that evening. Hugh put the quietus to this when he reminded us that this girl had been treated for a case of the crabs just a month or so back. The Pip remarked he might be willing to chance a case of the crabs in order to get laid. We all laughed at his comment, but the net effect of our conversation convinced us that there was a long, boring evening just lying in wait for us.

I propped up on one elbow and suggested that we ride into Macon and attend the Tuesday night wrestling matches. As y'all know, I love pro wrestling and have watched it for a number of years. Hugh's a big fan as well. There seemed to be some general consensus developing among the three of us that we would go. Once that was established, Hugh's mind shifted into overdrive, "What if we went down there and just cheered like hell for the bad guys?" he asked.

I replied, "It wouldn't mean much unless we had a big crowd with us. If we had a bunch of guys there, we could blast the roof off the place!"

Hugh said, "Well, that's what we need to do then."

The three of us looked at each other and the light bulbs went on. We knew that the Macon pro wrestling crowd (mostly rural country folks—some came from counties miles away just to see it) didn't take kindly to people cheering for the bad guys. We knew if we did this we'd piss a lot of people off. And, we knew that to pull it off we'd have to take a lot of guys with us in order to avoid getting our asses whipped by some of the more irate fans in attendance. Ultimately, we knew that we were taking a very big risk for very little gain, other than to enjoy a few laughs.

I mentioned all these facts to my two brothers. After five seconds of serious thought, Hugh stated, "I'm in."

The Pip added, "Hell yes, let's go for it."

Thus decided, we began telling some of our buds in the dorm about our plan. The absurdity of it all, combined with the fact that there was nothing else to do, made it almost irresistible to them. Guys not only started volunteering to go, but they began recruiting even more guys to go on with us on this unique road trip.

By four that afternoon we had around sixty guys lined up to go. Hugh mentioned that we might want to try to get reservations at the Coliseum so that we could all sit together in one block of seats. I thought this was a good idea so we all scrambled over to the pay phone on our floor and called the Coliseum ticket office. The conversation went something like this . . .

"Coliseum Box Office. Can I help you?"

"Yes ma'am. My name is Ed Williams and I need to reserve some tickets for wrestling tonight."

"How many tickets will you need?"

"About sixty, ma'am."

"You must be kidding, young man. There's no way you can really need sixty tickets," she stated.

"Ma'am, I go to Georgia College and I have sixty guys who are ready to raise some hell tonight."

I went on to tell her, in great detail, about our plan and assured her that we were good for the tickets. She began laughing like crazy and said, "You boys must want to get killed. Hon', let me get the promoter."

The promoter was an old guy named Hot House Fred. Hot House had wrestled for a long time in the Georgia area until he got too obese to step through the ring ropes. He was on the phone with me after I'd waited about a minute or so.

"Boy, are y'all serious about doing this?" he asked.

"Yes, sir, we are," I replied.

"Y'all do know that if you raise a lot of hell down here that you're gonna get this crowd really pissed off. Lots of people believe this shit is real."

"That's the whole reason we want to go, sir. My friend Hugh is doing a college term paper on crowd psychology and we need to do this thing as sort of a classroom experiment," I stated.

"Son, I know yer bullshittin' me, but if you limp dicks are serious about doing this, I'll hold you a whole row of ringside seats. The matches start at eight, but y'all need to be here by seven 'cause I can't hold them any longer than that."

I thanked Mr. Hot House and got off the phone. We were all rolling in the aisles laughing about the conversation in the hallway. Guys were talking about how much hell we were gonna raise, how much beer would be consumed, etc.

Ray looked up in the midst of all this and said, "One of us needs to wear a mask."

I stared at Ray and asked, "A mask? Why?"

"Look—you have to take me with faith on this. Someone needs to wear a mask."

Mike Parks, who would do anything and typically had a blood alcohol count higher than the Empire State Building, stepped forward and volunteered to don the mask. The Pip smiled, looked at Mike, and said, "You're gonna be the luckiest man here tonight, Mike."

Mike thanked Ray for this honor and we all went on about our business for the rest of the afternoon. We ate dinner together early in the evening so that we could be sure we left for Macon on time. I think we left around six P.M. or so. We really must have looked like a funeral procession because of all the cars we took—there had to be nine or ten of them lined up when we left. We made it to Macon without incident and noted that the Coliseum parking lot was already filling up when we got there. This was not unusual as on the average Tuesday night around eight to nine thousand people attended these wrestling matches.

Brother Foskey stepped out of the lead vehicle (the one carrying all three members of the Brotherhood) and remarked that it was going to be a special night, "There's no way this can't be good. Look at the crowd we have to work with, E." (At this point Hugh motions towards a guy in a tie-dyed t-shirt with about one-third of his cellulite rippled gut hanging out. Accompanying him was his wife, who had to be wider than Kate Smith and Roseanne put together).

I had to admit that Hugh was on to something. What he and I and the rest of us knew was mostly rural country people attended the pro wrestling matches. They were good people, but some were under educated and most swore that pro wrestling was a legitimate sport. Because of this, it was very easy for some of them to get major pissed at some of the shenanigans going on in the ring.

We disembarked from our cars and walked up to one of the ticket windows. Hugh stepped right up from the crowd and informed the ticket seller that he was there to pick up sixty ringside tickets. When he said that, the gal in the ticket booth started laughing pretty hard. After she calmed down she looked at all of us, smiled, and said, "Y'all must be those boys from Georgia College." She laughed some more and added, "I'll give y'all this—you may get your asses whipped tonight but y'all have balls bigger than a whale's."

We were all taken slightly aback at this as none of us had a clue as to the size of a whale's genitalia. We did sort of congratulate ourselves on the idea that we must be pretty brave to do what we were about to do. These noble thoughts got interrupted when the ticket agent said, "Y'all need to go speak to Mr. Fred (Hot House). He wants to talk to y'all before you go to your seats."

This scared us a little as Mr. Hot House was fatter than an irregular hippo and appeared to have the IQ of a hot sack of biscuits. We deduced his IQ was less than Einstein-like from having observed him doing interviews during the televised wrestling programs. He mispronounced words like *fists*, *work-out*, and *fight*, and conducted half the interviews with a chaw of Red Man in his mouth. Whatever our opinions of his mental abilities, our group trudged on back to his office, which had "Hot House Fred—Assistant Promoter" inscribed on the door.

We walked in and just stood there mutely. Hot House's secretary, who had bleached blonde hair and breasts like missile silos, smiled and said, "Y'all must be those college boys."

Brother Pippin, who's been known to flirt with a woman with a prime body and low IQ, replied, "Yes, and aren't you that woman that played Ginger on Gilligan's Island?"

The Ginger clone laughed and said, "No cutie, that wasn't me, but thanks for thinkin' so. Mr. Fred is ready to see y'all now."

She motioned us towards his door and Ray, Hugh, and I stepped inside, the other attendees right behind us. Hot House was sitting behind his desk chewing Red Man, and making out the line-up for the next Tuesday night's wrestling card. He looked up at us and said, "You boys know what you're getting into? Some of these people believe this silly shit is real."

We assured him we did, and Hot House continued, "Y'all raise some first class hell tonight. It'll get this place rockin' and rollin'. Based on what I'm seeing, there ought to be about eight thousand or so people here tonight. I did tell the cops on duty to sorta keep an eye on things, just in case some of these folks decide to whip y'all's asses."

"Mr. Fred," I spoke up, "they'll have to be damn brave. There are almost sixty of us here."

"I like yer thinkin', boy. Y'all have a damn good time tonight." And with that, he motioned us out of his office.

As we strolled back out Brother Pippin winked and said goodbye to Miss Ginger. She looked up and said a return goodbye, and then she noticed the ski mask-disguised Mike Parks. She looked back at Ray and asked, "Why is he wearing that?"

The Pip said that modesty forbade him to say. She tried again, "Tell me—why is he wearing that damn mask? Is he trying to be a wrestler?"

Ray looked at her and said, "Do you really want the truth?"

We figured she did, and she proved it by nodding. The Pip leaned over and whispered, "He's got the biggest trouser cobra at Georgia College. On account of that, he's fairly well known in this area. If we don't put a mask on him, we can never get any peace and quiet when we go somewhere. The women won't leave him alone."

Miss Ginger gaped and then whispered, "You're bullshitting me."

Ray told her he was not and told her to discreetly glance at Mike's crotch. She did that and gasped out loud. What she didn't know was earlier Mike had tied a toilet paper core around his pink crusader in order to give it that John Holmes look. Ray said that it was hard to be serious as he saw the expression on her face as she quickly visually inventoried Mike's crotch.

"That damn boy is hung like a horse!" Miss Ginger purred.

Ray told her that Mike had delivered screwings to some area women that had put 'em in the hospital. The receptionist laughed, and I'm sure she didn't believe us, but she kept staring at Mike's trouser-covered hydrant. I interrupted her hypnotic state when I told the guys that we all needed to get to our seats. We proceeded to leave the office, and I swear that Miss Ginger watched Mike's every step as he walked out the door.

Ray, Hugh, and I led the way to ringside. We were real early, and yet there was already a considerable crowd gathered inside the Coliseum. We figured we would get an early beer, sit back, ogle the crowd for nice-looking women, and wait for the matches to begin.

The minutes passed, and the time for the matches to get underway was drawing near. You could sense this by watching some of the crowd's antics. People were whistling loud, some were stomping their feet, and one guy in overalls broke a rather noisy flatus to indicate his readiness for the action to begin. Finally, the ring announcer walked up to the mike and said, "Ladies and gentlemen, welcome to the Macon Coliseum for a night of NWA Georgia Championship Wrestling!"

The crowd roared like Elvis had just walked in. When the applause died down, the announcer asked us to rise for the playing of the national anthem. You know, I'm very patriotic, but I've always wondered why the national anthem is played right before some guys are about to whip each others' asses. It seems just a bit strange, you know. It's like the crowd is saying, "Let's be patriotic and express our love for our country before these guys beat the hell out of each other." Even with those thoughts dancing through my head, I was still fully patriotic. All sixty-some-odd of us Georgia College boys stood up with pride when the first notes of the anthem rang out, and we all put our hands over our hearts. At the conclusion of the national anthem the crowd cheered mightily. One voice in the crowd was heard to yell, "Let's see some major ass-kickings tonight!"

With the mood appropriately set, we sat down and waited for the first combatants of the evening to make their appearances. For those of you who aren't familiar with pro wrestling, the matches always start out with the most unknown wrestlers grappling first. This is due to the fact that if the best ones came out initially, the crowd would go home after their matches—and the wrestling promoters can't have that. The preliminary wrestlers—often referred to as *jobbers* because their job is to lose in a way that makes the big-name wrestlers look good—develop into bigger names if they can wrestle and interview well. So, the promoters use them both to pad the card and as their "farm system" to develop future main-event wrestlers.

It didn't take long for a murmur to pass through the crowd. A masked man was walking out to the ring. He was the heavy for the first match, (or *heel*, in wrestling parlance) and his name was "El Diablo" or something similar to that. None of us had ever heard of him, and he was physically very small. Even Hugh whispered to me that he thought he could whip his ass. All of us didn't really give a damn about any of that, though. What did matter was that this man was the heel, and we had collectively agreed to cheer the heels. We all looked at each other and, as if on cue, we rose from our seats and started cheering for this guy. In a few seconds we were hollering for him like crazy, urging him to win the match and to break whatever rules he needed to in order to win. When he heard this, he literally stopped walking to the ring and stared at us. Then, he smiled and waved, and bounded up the steps to get into the ring and begin his match.

When he got inside the ring, we started hollering for him all over again. It was so loud (sixty of us, remember) that even the referee looked over at us and smiled. The cops stationed at ringside seemed to be enjoying our emotional outbursts, too. There were four of them, one each stationed at each corner of the ring, and they were all laughing. In fact, one officer was laughing so hard he had his handkerchief out and was dabbing the corners of his eyes. It was good for us that those cops were enjoying our yelling 'cause the rest of the crowd was stonily silent. In fact, more than a few of the folks in attendance were starting to stare in our direction. I mentioned this observation to both Hugh and the Pip—Ray said that we all enjoyed freedom of speech in America, and, "E. do you really think these sod farmers are gonna come down here and start some shit with sixty of us eyeing their asses?"

I couldn't refute that sound logic. Anyway, the crowd noise picked up again and the good guy ("babyface" in wrestling parlance) approached the ring. He was supposed to be a French guy named Rene Goulet and he'd wrestled for a lot of years. His hairline was shot to hell, but his trunks diverted your attention from that shortcoming. They were the deepest shade of red and made his ass look somewhat like a traffic light.

The ref motioned El Diablo and Rene Goulet to the center of the ring. As he gave them instructions, we hollered remarks into the ring. Stuff like, "Don't watch our man too close, ref."

"Rene looks sort of sweet, ref. If he tries to kiss El Diablo, disqualify his ass."

Other such niceties followed. Soon, both combatants returned to their corners to get ready for the match to begin. El Diablo turned around and looked as he walked back to his corner. He saw that Goulet was also returning to his and had his back to him. Like a panther, El Diablo ran across the ring and whacked Goulet across the back with a forearm. All of us Georgia College guys rose to our feet at this terrible display of sportsmanship, and we cheered our man mightily.

El Diablo dropped Goulet to the mat with another forearm. Then he started putting the boots to him. Kick after kick rained down upon the fallen Frenchman. It was great—a major ass-kicking and our man was the one opening up a can of whup-ass. Hugh even stood up and tried to get the referee to call the match because he was concerned Goulet was gonna get killed. All of us laughed pretty hard when he hollered that sentiment, and then we all started urging the ref to stop the match. The ref smiled at us a couple of times, but no dice. The match continued.

Goulet looked about done when, on his knees and hurting, he gave our man El Diablo a forearm between his legs that looked like a direct shot to the balls. Whatever it was, it dropped our masked man like an anchor. All of us guys stood up and protested like hell to the ref about this blatant cheating, but it did no good. The ref didn't see the illegal balls shot, and tolled out the three count on El Diablo.

At this point in the evening's festivities, I knew that we must be getting a rise out of the crowd. People were flipping us the bird when the ring announcer proclaimed Goulet's victory. We booed like hell and hollered mercilessly at the ref for his poor handling of the match. Even he was laughing at us, and those poor ringside cops were beside themselves. Ray was questioning the ref's parentage, and Brother Foskey and I were offering moral support to the still unsteady El Diablo. He sorta nodded thanks at us as he left the ring, holding his head with one hand and his mauled balls with the other.

Based on how the crowd had just treated us, we three resolved to really let them have it from there on out. There would be no holding back in upcoming matches—we were gonna yell till our throats hurt. The Pip was the most indignant, "Imagine laughing at a man who just took a shot to the balls. We've got to even this shit up, E. The honor of the Brotherhood demands it."

When the Pip said that, Hugh and I both got real serious. Our pride had just been assailed by this crowd. I think we were all pondering just what exactly to do when Hugh said, "Wonder if we should lighten up just a little bit? These people seem pretty pissed off."

Brother Pippin didn't even hesitate a second in responding, "Hugh, do we really give a rat's ass? Don't we have a right to say what we want? These dim bulbs need to lighten up—it's a damn wrestling match, for chrissakes."

Nothing else needed be said after that. Hugh and I both agreed that we were going the limit with this. Ray even added that it might back 'em off more if we really laid into 'em when the next match came out.

About this time, someone walked up to one of the ringside cops, who in turned walked over to where Ray, Hugh, and I sat. As he approached us, he asked, "Is there a Mike Parks here with y'all?"

Ray replied that he was with our group and was sitting a few seats down from us. We also told the officer that he couldn't miss him as he was wearing a ski mask. The policeman looked and spotted Mike, who was sitting there quietly and just happened to be drunker than a cockroach in a mayonnaise jar.

"Is Mike in some kind of trouble, Officer?" I asked.

"No, son. They want to speak with him up in the front office," he replied.

Both Ray and I were both puzzled as hell at this turn of events. We couldn't imagine what they would want Mike for up in the front office. As it turned out, we just stood there and watched the policeman walk over and speak a few words to him. Following that, Mike got up and followed the officer up the inclined steps of the Coliseum.

We would have paid more attention to Mike, and we did sort of look for him over the next couple of matches, but we never spotted him. To be honest, we sort of stopped looking when they announced that the semifinal match of the evening was about to begin. Catcalls and nasty language rang out as Abdullah the Butcher began making his way to the ring. Abdullah was a huge black man, who was supposed to be from the Sudan. Actually, a rumor had floated around for years that he lived in Conyers and even dabbled a bit in goat farming.

We heard the murmur from the crowd and spotted Abdullah slowly approaching the ring. We all got up and cheered him mightily. As he walked towards the ring, he looked over at us and raised his elbow up in the air. This was the gesture he used before he dropped his devastating elbow smash on an opponent. No one ever got up from Abdullah's elbow smashes.

The finger pointing and catcalls from the crowd were getting much worse. I actually saw a group of middle-aged women sitting together who simultaneously flipped us all the bird. We laughed like hell at 'em and, on the count of three, saluted them with our upraised middle fingers. The boos that erupted from this were far worse than anything we had experienced to that point in the evening. We really did have this crowd going—so much so that one of the police officers on duty at ringside was laughing to the point that he was bent over in his chair.

A look to our left revealed a large contingent of Boy Scouts. Apparently, several local troops were in attendance that night. One of the Scout masters, in full uniform, walked over to us and said, "Do you realize that you're setting a bad example for these boys?"

Brother Pippin quickly responded by saying, "Do you think I'm gonna take advice from a grown man who's wearing a handkerchief around his neck?"

We all laughed and continued on with our taunting of the crowd.

Back to the match—Abdullah was now in the ring and the fans were hurling lots of negative comments at him. Abdullah seemed not to be fazed by this at all; in fact, we almost thought he was smiling at us a couple of times when we really hollered loudly for him.

The taunts and catcalls aimed at Abdullah abruptly ended as his opponent was seen making his way to the ring. On this particular evening, Wildfire Tommy Rich was Abdullah's adversary.

Wildfire Tommy Rich had to be only about seventeen or eighteen years old when this particular match took place. At that time, he was very slender and had a mop of bleached-out blond hair. The women in the crowd absolutely adored him. I think they sort of lusted for him and wanted to mother him at the same time. Whatever the attraction was, these women sure loved him. He was definitely the wrestling heartthrob of the seventies era for Georgia Championship Wrestling.

The crowd was really letting us guys have it good. Taunts like, "You baggers better bend over and get ready" or "Tommy's gonna chew Abdullah's ass up like a dog does a bone" were among the many hurled at us. You have to remember this about a rural southern wrestling crowd in the seventies—they took a loss by one of their favorites as a personal insult. To them, the Tommy/Abdullah match personified a good Southern boy going up against a wicked foreign man. If you were for anyone else other than the good Southern boy, you had to be as wicked as Abdullah himself!

You could tell that this match was going to be an interesting one right from the get-go. The festivities began when, during the ref's instructions to the wrestlers, Abdullah kicked Tommy in the stomach. When Tommy bent over from the blow, Abdullah yanked his warm-up jacket over his head and started beating the hell out of him. The ref quickly signaled the timekeeper to go ahead and ring the bell to begin the match.

The crowd was already insane with rage. This worsened when Abdullah proceeded to drag Tommy around the ring by his jacket. When Tommy tried to escape, Abdullah grabbed his hair and proceeded to drag him around some more. This made all the women go crazy as they drooled over Tommy Rich's bleached blond hair. Abdullah further offended their sensibilities when he backed Rich into a corner. When the referee ordered the two wrestlers to break, Abdullah leaned over and bit Tommy's nose. He bit it so hard that blood started gushing out of it like the foam off a south Georgia river. What made this even more inflammatory for the fans was the fact that Abdullah spit out into the crowd after he bit Wildfire's nose. This was sort of like telling the fans that Tommy Rich was so dirty that you'd spit after you had ingested a piece of him.

Being the discreet guys that we were, we were all visibly howling with laughter over this turn of events. We would hold our noses and feign great pain, openly mocking the now-suffering Tommy Rich. We kept asking each other for ketchup to go with Tommy's nose. One thing for sure, we were doing a damn good job of keeping the crowd riled up. It's a wonder we hadn't already gotten into some kind of physical altercation with some of these highly incensed fans.

Lo and behold, Tommy began to get his second wind and started fighting back. He kicked Abdullah in the midsection and bent him over. Then, he climbed up on the second turnbuckle and hit him with a solid forearm across the back. Abdullah dropped to the mat like Marilyn Chambers from the blow.

The crowd was now roaring its approval. People were looking over at us and yelling, "What do you shitheads think now?" or "Like that ass-whupping? Tommy's got some more for you!" We were all impressed with the eloquence and originality of the remarks, and applauded openly when some of the better ones were made.

These remarks went into hyperdrive when Tommy started jumping up in the air and landing with his fist firmly planted in the middle of Abdullah's forehead. He did this over and over and over—so many times that the crowd was counting them off. "Five . . . six . . . seven . . ." went the chant as Tommy Rich's fist found the mark squarely on Abdullah's forehead again and again.

From where the Brotherhood was sitting, we could see that Abdullah was beginning to bleed rather badly. Of course, this pumped the crowd up greatly as they figured it was now only a matter of time before the evil Abdullah was conquered and Tommy Rich could claim his rightful victory.

The Brotherhood always fights to the last breath whenever faced with a challenge. We weren't about to do anything different in this particular situation, either. I guess we figured that if we were all going down, we were gonna go down hard. We got the guys to all stand up and cheer like crazy for Abdullah. We called out to the ref that Tommy Rich was cheating. We hollered this so much that the ref even checked Tommy's hands to be sure he wasn't using a foreign object against our beloved Sudanese Butcher.

After this happened, Rich turned, looked at us, and said, "I'm really gonna bust his head now."

We hollered our thanks to Tommy for displaying such sharpened grammatical skills, but, however bad his grammar, Tommy was as good as his word. He started hammering Abdullah with a barrage of hard right hands to the head. He didn't let up, either—Tommy must have bounced his gourd with right hands for a good ten minutes or so.

Finally, the ref backed him off Abdullah. I figured our man was gonna stay down on the mat and ultimately lose the match. This turned out not to be the case—Abdullah somehow managed to struggle up to his feet. He was wobbly as hell, but he did stand up. Tommy Rich saw this and ran right by the ref to keep whuppin' up on Abdullah.

This is the point in the match where Tommy Rich made a critical mistake. When he ran over to attack Abdullah, the man from the Sudan dropped him with a hard chop to his Adam's apple. Rich fell over like a drunk on a freshly waxed floor. Being the consummate sportsman, Abdullah walked over, grabbed Tommy by the hair, and pulled him to his feet.

As Rich got yanked into a standing position, the ref's attention was diverted by the ringside timekeeper. Noticing this, Abdullah pulled his opponent over to the corner closest to us guys. Looking directly at us and smiling, the Butcher pulled a pencil out of his trunks. Then, nodding to us and smiling even more broadly, he proceeded to give Tommy Rich three to four good shots to the throat with the pencil. Rich dropped like a politician spying loose change on the sidewalk.

All of us guys proceeded to go hog-ass wild—we hollered and screamed like banshees for our man, Abdullah. Abdullah nodded at us again, backed into the ropes, and landed the Sudanese elbow drop right into the middle of Tommy Rich's chest.

"One . . . two . . . three," came the count from the referee. The match had ended, and our man Abdullah had won!

At that moment, if Elvis Presley himself had walked into the Coliseum, he wouldn't have gotten as big a hand as the one we gave Abdullah. We yelled, cheered, stomped, and hollered like a bunch of madmen for him. A few of us even made toasts to the victory, using cups of cold brewskis.

We failed to notice in the midst of all this merriment the somber silence that engulfed the entire Coliseum. The vast majority of the fans in attendance were stunned and, if you think about it, why shouldn't they be? Tommy Rich had been kicking Abdullah's ass for fifteen minutes and lost the match? How could that have possibly happened?

"I'll tell you how it happened!" one lady screamed out. "Those stickdicks over there helped distract the ref! They caused Tommy to lose!"

It didn't take anymore than that to convince this crowd that we were responsible. Of course, Hugh did the only decent thing and yelled over to the woman that he wouldn't screw her with a dead man's dick. That comment got us a laugh or two, but strangely enough, didn't appear to help us out a whole bunch. The damage had been done. This crowd was mega-pissed at all sixty-some-odd of us Abdullah supporters.

The boos and catcalls weren't so bad. The challenges we got from some of the fans in attendance were. One nice-looking young blonde, maybe twenty years of age, ran right up to Hugh and me. Her face was beet red, she had tears streaming down her face, and her fists were clenched. As she stormed up to us, she said, "I'll get in the ring with any one of you bastards and kick your asses right now!"

To this loving comment I replied, staring directly into her chest, "That's probably the best offer Hugh and I've had all day."

This young lady was not amused. She drew back her fist, and I swear she was gonna smack us until she noticed a ringside cop rising from his chair and walking over in our direction. Fearful of arrest, she contented herself by making comments to us about how we couldn't have possibly been raised in decent homes. She also added that the least we could do was keep our ignorance to ourselves. I think she was about to say more when the police officer came over and escorted her back to her seat. As she left us, she sneered and flipped us stereo birds.

We had no time to ponder all this because a fossilized old man walked up right after she left. He was wearing a grimy pair of overalls and a t-shirt and appeared to not have shaved in the last week or so. Of course, these negative qualities were offset by the fact that he had several good teeth in his head, and breath that made a meat house's scrap heap smell like half a dozen roses. He looked Hugh, Ray, and me right in the eyes and said, "Y'all are the scum of the earth!"

Amongst all of us Hugh especially seemed to want to laugh like hell, but manners dictated we not do so directly into the old man's face. After a moment or so of reflection, Hugh put on his best pensive facial expression and said, "Sir, are you addressing your remarks to us?"

The old man looked like he didn't comprehend what Hugh was saying.

Hugh got a bit louder, "Sir, were you talking to us?"

The old man caught this remark and replied, "No asshole, I was talking to that row of chairs back there."

Now, of course, these could be interpreted as fighting words. And so it would be with most of the people in this world. But, this is the Brotherhood, and we're a different breed. Hell, we're the most elite social organization in the world.

Given that, there was no point in egging this mush-headed old fellow on. As Ray so eloquently pointed out to Hugh, "If you kick his ass, what have you done? Laid out some old gap-toothed bastard that smells bad? That's not even worth the effort it would take."

That logic was indisputable, so Brother Foskey kindly told the man that he would ignore what he had just said. He then told him to take his seat as he was a paying customer and there was one match left to observe. For some reason, I guess because of the way Hugh said that, we all started laughing. The old man thought he had just been sassed, so he pointed his finger right at Hugh and said, "Which of you boys wants his ass whupped first?"

Hugh paused before he answered, which was good, as that was all the time it took for one of the ringside cops to come over. "Is there any problem here?" the officer inquired.

Hugh looked directly at the old man and said, "Repeat what you just said, you rank-ass old gaffer."

The old man got red-faced and yelled, "I told this young sonofabitch that I was about to kick his ass. And I'm gonna—"

With that, he lunged at Hugh. Of course, the police officer easily subdued the enraged geriatric and took him right out of the building. The only problem was that lots of people witnessed this episode, and it looked like we had just gotten his tired old ass kicked out of the building.

A chant went up from the crowd that started gaining momentum, "Georgia College sucks! Georgia College sucks!" The crowd was letting us know, in no uncertain terms, that they didn't like us and pretty much wanted to stake our dead carcasses to fire ant mounds. Hugh, Ray, and I looked at them for awhile, then, we began smiling at the most vehement chanters.

The hubbub died down a little as everyone waited for the main-event match of the evening. It was to be a one-fall encounter between Ol' Anderson and Thunderbolt Patterson. As it got closer to time for it to begin, one of the ringside cops walked over and motioned to Hugh, Ray, and me to follow him towards the back of the building. We got up and did as he said, although we were confused as hell as to what he wanted with us.

When we got about twenty feet of so away from the crowd, the officer started laughing. "I just wanted to tell you boys—I have to come out here every Tuesday night and work security for this shit. Most nights, it's so damn boring you can't believe it. Tonight, for the first time, I'm glad I wasn't anywhere else. I haven't laughed like this in a long, long time."

We thanked the officer for allowing us to provide him with some good entertainment. He nodded and smiled, but then went on to add, "There is one problem, though."

"What is that, sir?" Ray replied.

"Let's just say that y'all have managed, in a couple of hours, to get this crowd more riled up than a pissed-on yellow jackets' nest."

"Yes, we've noticed that, sir," I answered.

"The reason I took y'all over here is that I wanted to show you the back exit out of the Coliseum. I don't mean to alarm you, but when this last match ends y'all need to leave using this door. If you don't, and decide to leave with the rest of these people, they are going to kill you. And I ain't kiddin'. These people are madder than hell. It's best you go out the back way as soon as this match is over. Don't mess around—get out."

We all gulped and looked at each other, but nodded to the officer that we would do as he asked. The three of us then went back out and took our seats. Of course, when sixty of your friends see a police officer leading you away, it stimulates a whole lot of questioning. All the guys crowded around, wanting to know what had just transpired.

The Pip told them, "We've had fun here tonight, but a lot of these people take this shit seriously. Simply put, they all want to whip our asses when this last match is over. I think we can whip some of them, but there's no way in hell that we can lick eight thousand of them. The officer showed us the back way out of here, and soon as this match is over, that's where we need to be headed."

For the first time during the course of the evening, the hilarity and lightheartedness ended. We realized that we had taken something cherished to these people and rubbed their noses in it. We had taken the low road, cheering for the heels while the good wrestlers were being flagrantly abused. And, we had openly condoned all this cheating. I think I spoke for all the group when I said to Ray, "I guess we had all better shut up and watch this last match in silence."

Ray listened to my statement, and his eyes immediately widened. In less than a second he responded, "Silence, my pale white ass! We've paid our money tonight to watch this wrestling. And, we have every right to cheer for who we want to. That's why our forefathers fought for our freedoms—so that we could express ourselves! And we will express ourselves, even if these dick-headed Neanderthals see it another way."

All of us stared at Ray in complete amazement. You could almost sense the admiration from the group for his position in this matter—lots of heads were nodding and there were several knowing smiles. You had to admire his spirit, courage, and determination. He didn't end by just stating this, though. He added one more point which told me all I needed to know, "E. you're a member of the Brotherhood. Will we let these used tampons stop us from having a good time?"

Now you know damn well how I answered that. Ray was right, as he typically is. And his point was very well-made. In the Brotherhood, you set the standards, not adhere to someone else's. We had done nothing wrong here. Plus, if we slunk off like we'd had our asses whipped, it would send a bad example to anyone that wanted to exercise their right to cheer for the bad guys in the future.

Ray set the tone when he hollered out to Ol' Anderson, "Whip this fag!" Lots of eyes turned and focused on him, including both Ol' Anderson's and Thunderbolt Patterson's.

And, to not be outdone, Hugh looked out at the crowd, held his middle finger up high in the air and said, "Smoke this filter tip, you pink-assed monkey look-alikes!"

I thought the cops at ringside were going to go into convulsions. The officer who talked to us was laughing so hard that his face resembled the color of pickled beets. Another officer on the opposite side of the ring was laughing and openly talking about his need to go to the bathroom. Our whole group, after observing these policemen, started laughing like hell right along with them. Funny thing was, we didn't figure we could piss this crowd off any worse than we already had. But we did—even though I was convinced that we couldn't.

We had guys hollering insults at us about our mothers, and one guy got escorted out when he threw a cup of Co-Cola towards us. We further inflamed the situation by hollering encouragements to the officer leading the guy out.

"Get his ass out of here. Law-abiding citizens wish to enjoy these matches!"

"Man, that guy's ugly. He could model for hemorrhoid advertisements!"

Since he didn't hit us: "With an arm like that, Catfish Hunter must be sweatin'!"

We said all these things and more. By that point, we had set ourselves up for a lynching. These people weren't even hollering now—they were very solemn-faced and kept staring at us. Ray leaned over and whispered, "We need to knock it off. Fun is fun but let's get the hell out of here."

I passed the message along, and, as fate would have it, the match ended at this point anyway. If I remember correctly, Thunderbolt Patterson pinned Ol' Anderson and the crowd immediately went crazy with excitement. We didn't waste time, though. Ray said that we needed to get the hell out, and Hugh and I quickly agreed. The three of us jumped over our seats, and headed like minks with the trots towards the back exit.

The other guys saw us leaving and proceeded to follow us out the back door. I don't think the general crowd noticed us too much at that point as they were engrossed in cheering Thunderbolt Patterson on his big victory. Thunderbolt kept 'em even more occupied by taking a chair and bouncing it off Ol' Anderson's head two or three times. This caused 'em to raise the rafters even more.

As this touching scene played out inside, sixty or so college boys were outside running around the outer perimeter of the Coliseum. We were all jumping over shrubs, trashcans and God knows what else in our haste to get to our cars. As is typical in high-stress situations like this, one guy in our group got winded and couldn't keep up. He sort of fell to one knee and was breathing heavily. Seeing this, a couple of his buddies tried to drag him along, but he insisted that he had to rest a minute. This rest period ended when Brother Foskey ran over and said, "If you don't get your ass up, you'll have eternity to rest! Either hustle those pink apples up, or find another way home. We're getting the hell out of here!"

It can never be said that Brother Foskey doesn't tell it like it is. We all turned and started running again. The guy in question decided that being out of breath temporarily was a better option than being out of it permanently, so, he got his cellulite buns up and hustling towards the cars, too.

We finally made it out into the main parking lot and were zigzagging between rows of cars as we frantically ran to ours. As we all got closer to our metallic salvations, the Pip hollered out, "What about Parks?"

We all slowed down when he said that. Parks? We had forgotten about him in the midst of all the excitement. Then I got to thinking. We hadn't seen Parks at all after the policeman had come and gotten him, roughly about halfway through the matches. I genuinely began to get worried. What had happened to Mike? Was he all right? Would he get beaten up if he came out and discovered that, in our haste, we had left him? Should we hang around and wait for him to show his face?

There wasn't time to wait. As we got closer to our cars, people were coming out of the Coliseum in droves. We saw some of them look in our general direction and point at us. We scrambled like hell for our cars, but, we could already hear some pretty unnerving comments.

"There's those smart-ass bastards! Let's see how they like a real, sho-nuff ass-whuppin'!"

"We need to stomp a mud hole for what they did to poor Tommy Rich!"

"I may go to jail but I'm gettin' my money's worth out of their hides!"

All these things were said and more. After hollering their find out to all the people leaving the Coliseum, some of the ringleaders started walking over in our direction. Brother Pippin set our future course of action quickly, "Screw Parks! If we don't get the hell out of here now, Parks will be visiting all of us in the funeral home."

Nothing else needed be said—everyone began scrambling into their cars. As Ray, Hugh, and I sighted our vehicle, we noticed that it was moving up and down slightly, and all the windows were fogged up. We didn't have time to be polite and knock—we threw the door to the car open and quickly solved the mystery of what was going on inside. For right there, in the back seat of our car, screwing their brains out like two rabbits on Viagra, were Parks and Miss Ginger!

Mike was totally oblivious to us opening the car door behind him. And, of course, it was less than aesthetically pleasing for the three of us to observe this tender scene—we open our car door and are greeted with Park's pimpled and hairy ass bobbing up and down in front of our faces. As Brother Pippin so aptly put it, "Makes you want to go and eat a sandwich, don't it?"

Hugh and I busted out laughing, which caused Mike to stop sinking the Bismarck and look over his shoulder, "What in the hell are y'all doing here?"

That question was never answered, as I noticed the group of guys I mentioned earlier was now less than thirty yards away, and bearing down on us. We did the only thing we could do—Ray jumped in the front seat and fired up the engine, I pulled Miss Ginger out and deposited her on the grass right next to the car, and Hugh dumped her clothes in her lap. Then, we proceeded to shag out of that parking lot like the Roadrunner with his ass on fire.

As we made our Burt Reynolds-type escape, I turned around and looked. Dumping Miss Ginger had helped us out a good bit. The group of guys that was bearing down on us stopped dead in their tracks when they saw her. I wouldn't doubt they thought they were hallucinating or something—a naked blonde in the grass at a parking lot? At a wrestling match? Whatever they were thinking, it stopped them dead in their tracks. I did notice a policeman walking over into the rapidly gathering crowd. It sure would have been interesting to hear what Miss Ginger had to say to that cop, but we were speeding away and making tracks back to Milledgeville.

We wheeled out on old Gray Highway and began catching our collective breaths. Ray immediately began reprimanding Parks for "smelling like a bowl of groin soup." Of course, we did congratulate him on his conquest, but, we still had to tell him that his body odor was somewhat like that of a dried frog's corpse. Parks laughed pretty hard, and proceeded to give us the touching story of his erotic encounter.

It seems that Brother Pippin's remarks about the size of Parks's love missile had made a big impression on Miss Ginger, so much so that she had one of her buddies on the police force go down and fetch him from the Coliseum crowd. Parks said he was worried at first that he'd done something wrong, but he found the cop to be reassuring and even laughing as they walked up to Hot House Fred's office.

Once inside Hot House's office, Parks saw that Miss Ginger was seated behind her desk. He also noted that her blouse was unbuttoned all the way down to her navel, and, she had on enough lipstick to insure that her lips would not have been harmed even if she had French kissed a knife blade.

Parks said that she got up from her desk, walked right up to him, and grasped his love handle "like she was 'bout to throw a knuckleball." This took Parks aback, but he let nature take its course and began lip-lockin' with her. After a few minutes of that, Parks said that he was more than ready to get horizontal. Apparently, Miss Ginger felt the same as, after a two-minute duel of tongues, she suggested they leave the office and find someplace to "do nature's deed." Parks, who was higher than the Wallendas at this point, told her that he was broke and the back seat of our car would have to do. He said that this ol' gal was so hot that she would have agreed to do it on top of a septic tank. She threw on an over-coat and the two of them made their way out to the parking lot and, ultimately, into the back seat of our car. Parks said when the two of them got in the back seat that things went pretty well until she took her bra off. It wasn't that she didn't have nice boobs—we all saw how magnifi-cent they were when we tossed her out of the car. The bad thing was that her bra had enough wire in it to reinforce the underside of the Golden Gate Bridge. Parks said that when she whipped it off, a corner of it caught him in the eye and scratched his eyeball pretty badly. Mike shot up out of the seat and held his head, which was now throbbing with pain. Miss Ginger sat up as well and tried to comfort him. Mike said that his eye was hurting like a bitch, but that this woman was too far gone. She had to have a man, and right then! Mike said the pain began subsiding a little when she mistook a critical part of his anatomy for a Charm's Blow Pop. In his words, "You don't use your eye to hone with." It was right after this, as was he violating Miss Ginger, that all of us ran out to the car and ultimately lobbed her into the parking lot.

We all laughed heartily at this tender tale of true romance. Ray lamented all the way home that he had told Miss Ginger that Parks was "the man." He said if he'd known that Parks would get laid from the lie that he would have told it about himself. Of course, Hugh and I reminded him that we had interrupted Mike and that he had not had a chance to finish his business. Ray retorted that he would not have pro-longed the act in the backseat of a car and would already have skeeted by the time we'd all gotten there.

In the next few days, word spread all over the college about what we had done at the matches. Dr. Long, spiritual advisor to the Brotherhood, made us tell him the whole story at a business fraternity party several nights later. After hearing it and laughing, he proceeded to ask us how we had managed to escape with our lives. Hugh gave him this answer, "Dr. Long, if Mike hadn't been engaged in illicit sexual activities we could have gotten away much sooner. He degraded himself and our group, and that's what made it such a close call."

When Ray and I heard this, we fought back the monumental urge to burst out laughing. We couldn't believe that Brother Foskey made the comment with a straight face! After all, Dr. Long knew of many of our past escapades and would certainly have believed us capable of this one. When we mentioned this to Hugh, he reminded us that Parks was not there, and that there was no reason to cast doubts upon the morals of the Brotherhood. He went on to remind us, "Hell, I'm just a college kid, and it seemed like the right thing to do. Is Parks a member of the

Brotherhood? We protect our own, first. 'Sides, anyone can armchair quarterback something, E."

How can you dispute that sound logic? You can't—it's just another reason why Hugh is a member of the Brotherhood and almost everyone else isn't. It's that thoughtful, pensive quality of his—Hugh is the kind of guy who can puke in your backyard at the yearly Brotherhood Christmas celebration and not make you mad. I guess he's just gifted with an ability to explain his actions in such a way that you can't get upset with him.

A few days after the wrestling matches, we got a call from the promoter, Hot House Fred. I still don't know how he got our phone number at the dorm, but he did. He basically offered all of us free tickets to the following week's matches if we'd return and cheer like hell for the bad guys. Apparently, we riled up the fans so much that it was spurring additional ticket sales for their upcoming shows. Ray and I talked about it, but we concluded that the crowd would likely be armed and ready for us if we showed again. As he put it, "Do we want our parents to have to explain to people that we died making fun of people at a wrestling match?"

I didn't want to do that, and he didn't either. Thus ended our research into the behavior of pro wrestling crowds.

A month or so ago Hugh and I took our sons to see professional wrestling at the Macon Centreplex. As we walked inside the building, we looked around at the elaborate sets that were in place for the evening's matches. We also noticed the large crowds of people, as wrestling always sells out the Centreplex whenever it's in town. As we looked around the building, we both gradually turned until eventually we were facing each other. We couldn't help but smile, 'cause I knew what both of us were thinking. Hugh then brought closure to this whole experience when he said, "Ed, these people can holler tonight, but we both know it's not a piss in the bucket compared with how the Brotherhood can work a crowd."

He's right, you know.

Chapter 8
LET'S BE HONEST ABOUT
LITTLE LEAGUE

☽

Ed, that little shit in left field couldn't
hem one up in a bushel basket.
—a competitive Little League parent

I know over the years there have been legitimate claims of discrimination made by various groups of people in our society. We all
commonly think of people suffering discrimination because of things
like their race, sex, age, religion, or whatever.

This is all well and good, but there is a form of insidious discrimination that is going on in this country as we speak. In fact, it's been going
on for years. Bad thing about it is that it affects a lot of us, and we just
quietly keep it to ourselves, for it is not politically correct discrimination. The effects of it, however, are eating away at me, and I know it
affects others I care about as well. It is time to expose this cancerous discrimination—decency and the American way of life demand it.

The discrimination I'm referring to centers around Little League
baseball. It is directed at those of us who are the parents of players—
more specifically, the parents of kids who are decent or better-than-
average ball players.

Ours is a sad lot. We have to endure a lot of things for our athletic
kids. If you don't think that's the case, consider the average Little
League team. Typically, it looks something like this: of the nine starting
players, three can catch, hit, and throw the ball; two can do a couple of
these things and don't embarrass anyone; one can typically throw but
couldn't hem up a fly ball with a wicker basket; three could not play ball
if they had a motorcycle to run the bases with and a clothes hamper to
catch the ball in.

This is the situation the parents of the decent or better ballplayer endure game after game after game. As you watch the game and see the same kid strike out for the third time (twice with the bases loaded and two outs), you bite your fingers because you want to cuss so badly. When this happens during a critical juncture in the game, I get up and go to the concession stand for a few minutes.

The reason I go to the concession stand is that it's a safe refuge for all the parents of good Little League players. Here you can find refreshments and all the empathy you'll ever need. Witness this conversation I had a couple of weeks ago after the same kid muffed two easy fly balls that caused a net total of six runs to be scored against us.

Me: (mumbling) "He couldn't hem up the damn ball if his glove was a hammock."

Fellow Concession Stand Patron: "Is that the Sullivan kid?"

Me: "Yeah, do you know him?"

FCSP: "Know him? The little dweeb lost five games for us last year!"

Me: "Yeah, I can see why. He couldn't catch a ball if it was made out of candy bars."

FCSP: "Last year he did the same shit. A group of us got so scared when the end-of-season tournament began that we actually considered paying him not to show up for the games."

Me: (after laughing) "Well, we both know that wouldn't work."

FCSP: (not laughing) "No, but what did work was calling his house right before the first playoff game and telling him that he had won five hundred dollars worth of free sports equipment at the Macon Mall. We told him that the prize had to be claimed within the next hour, though."

Me: "You've got to be kidding."

FSCP: (still not laughing) "Am I smiling? You just watched him cough up six runs. Do you blame me?"

Me: (mumbling profusely) "Er . . . well . . . doncha think . . . hmm-mmm . . ."

FCSP: "We won that damn ballgame, incidentally. Lost the next one and got eliminated from the tournament because ol' Leadhands out there dropped a can of corn with the bases loaded."

Me: (lengthy silence)

FCSP: "You look like you're really thinkin'. Are you okay?"

Me: "Yeah, just wonderin' if he's forgotten about that phone call now."

This type of conversation helps the parent of the gifted Little

Leaguer feel better. Being at the concession stand also allows you the opportunity to mutter oaths and swear words that would probably get you deported if you said them in the stands. Nothing like questioning the dexterity skills and male chromosome count of a kid underneath your breath to make you feel relaxed, refreshed, and ready to endure the rest of the ballgame.

As you observe Little League games over time, you'll notice there is an interesting assortment of parental types there in the stands with you. In fact, the behavioral patterns of a lot of them are predictable based on what I've seen in the past. The following, then, is a quick primer on the types of parents you'll mingle with at a typical Little League game:

Type One—The Heavy Kid's Mom

Unfortunately, every team has a heavy kid. It's almost like life, death, or taxes—he's just there. We had one on our team a few years ago who actually would not play unless mama gave him a candy bar during the game. Besides the fact that this kid needed a candy bar like he needed herpes, it was distracting to hear his high pitched whine game after game, "Mom, I need some candy." I always wanted to pop his round, little ass every time he hollered that.

One interesting thing about the heavy kid's mom is she will almost always mistake girth for power. She'll make comments like, "If my Ralphie gets around on the ball you'll see it take off outta here!" or "With Ralphie's large frame, I know he'll hit the ball with authority." When I hear this stuff, I really want to stand up and say, "Ralphie is a tub of goo, and couldn't get around on the ball if we goosed him with a cattle prod." Of course if I did say this, I would probably be squashed as the heavy kid's mom is typically a large woman herself. But I sure think about saying it, though.

Another problem is that the heavy kid's mom often has a very misguided idea as to what position her kid should play. Even though he may have the mobility of a swollen walrus, she will insist that shortstop or center field is his natural position. I actually heard one kid's mom make the statement a couple of years ago that her son, "even with his large bones," was probably the fastest kid on the team. What made this even more laughable was the fact that the kid would be wheezing just on the run to first base when issued a walk. I guess parental love blinds a parent to the largely obvious.

In defense of the heavy kid, there is one advantage to having one on your team. A heavy kid always has a mom, and invariably she carries a nice assortment of snacks for Junior in her purse or carryall bag. Knowing that to be the case, I always position myself close to her late in the game when she finds out Junior is full and desires no more food. At that point, she just wants to unload the stuff so that she doesn't have to carry it any longer—that's when I make my move, and gracefully accept the free snacks offered.

In any event, the heavy kid's mom is a veritable angel compared with the next parental type.

Type Two— Socialist Mom

This mom espouses the principles of sportsmanship and fairness until you want to gag. She's the one who insists on equal amounts of playing time for each player. You can always count on her kid being a poor player—the parents of the good player don't typically have to discuss playing time as their kid always gets plenty. But the socialist mom drones on about the rules, character building, the "game of life," etc.

The socialist mom really annoys Ed Jr. As he puts it, "If you're not out there to win, why is there a damn scoreboard?" And he has a point— why are you out there if not to win? I figure life is gonna teach us that we can't be successful at everything. Do we do children a favor by sheltering them from that? And is a child really being helped by putting him or her into something that they don't have the skills for? Is continual failure good for the child's character or ego? I've witnessed a couple of really sad cases where the child is out there for the father to live out his athletic fantasies. In these situations, as you watch the child's face after they strike out or make an error, you wonder, "Is he or she really gaining anything from this experience?" I personally don't think they are at all.

Ed Jr. and I have come to the conclusion that the socialist mom should focus her energies on worrying about endangered species, wetlands, or the ozone layer. This would get her off the ball field, and the rest of us could then play the damn game to win. I will break down and give her one praise, though—she is generally polite in her dealings with others in the stands. A far cry from the . . .

Type Three—Hollerin' (but haven't taught my son anything) Dad

This is a regrettable prototype Little League parent. Usually, there are one or two on every team. They'll holler and raise hell on every play, and are quick to use facial expressions and phrases to indicate displeasure with the way kids other than theirs are playing. Most of the time they are easier on their own kids, but this is not always true. Sometimes they are just as obnoxious in their dealings with them.

The worst thing about the hollerin' dad is that he expends tons of energy at the game, but typically hasn't any to use in teaching his own kid the fundamentals he or she so desperately needs. To me, this is akin

90   ❰   ED WILLIAMS

to placing one's child on a shooting range—sooner or later the kid is gonna get a frozen rope hit at him or her, and could get hurt—maybe badly. Of course, for the hollerin' dad this is not important, as he will find something or someone to blame the situation on—the sun was in his kid's eyes, his glove was new, etc., etc.

The best antidote for the hollerin' dad is to hook him up with the socialist mom. If you get these two together, they'll go on for hours talking about winning versus sportsmanship. The discussions between them can get pretty heated, too. This is an actual one I heard at a ballgame one night.

HD: "Son, if the runner on second tries to come home, throw him out if it's hit to you. We only have a one run lead!"

SM: "Aren't you expecting way too much from your child? There's no way his little arm will get the ball home in time to throw out the runner."

HD: "That may be true for your child, but my son Farquartz throws 'em like an incoming missile."

SM: "We must be watching two different children. Farquartz has barely managed the throws into second. You are not being fair in your expectations of him."

HD: "Dammit, I know my own son better than anyone else. He can make that throw, I tell you!"

SM: "Not only can't he make it, you will ruin his self-esteem if you continue with your unrealistic expectations."

HD: (long string of curse words, some of them really good ones, too)

SM: "Now let's calm down and return to watching the game. I have some Greenpeace literature you can read if you need a calming diversion."

After this exchange, I thought this particular hollerin' dad resembled someone who had just eaten a bee-corpse sandwich. I thought for a couple of seconds that the top of his head might blow off. He finally did calm down a little, but quickly changed seats so that he was a good piece down from where the socialist mom was sitting.

The hollerin' dad does have a few things going for him, though. First of all, he keeps the bleachers relatively empty as no one wants to sit near him and hear his big yap running throughout the course of the game. This is good if you are badly in need of a place to sit down—there will always be plenty of space readily available next to a hollerin' dad.

A second good point is that the hollerin' dad will almost always make you laugh if you do one simple thing—ask him what athletic endeavors he pursued while going through school? You'll get several minutes of the best stammering and stalling techniques that you can imagine. The reason for this is that, nine times out of ten, the hollerin' dad did not play sports or was pitifully pathetic at playing them. This background causes him to want his son to be what he could not be—a good ballplayer, which doesn't make a helluva lot of sense but that's how it works for the hollerin' dad. He is best observed at a distance, and is an ideal target to sic the following parental type on.

Type Four—Bench Warmer's Mom

The bench warmer's mom is ideal to sic on the hollerin' dad because she'll never cave in to him. When the hollerin' dad launches into a tirade about a kid on the team, the bench warmer's mom will eagerly remind him of the specific gaffes that his own kid has made during the course of the season. This will drive the hollerin' dad crazy, because specifics about play, especially his own kid's play, are not something he can tolerate. Therein lies the best point about the bench warmer's mom—she quiets down the hollerin' dad.

This good point aside, the bench warmer's mom can be a very bitter pill to take. There's not a lot of difference between her and the socialist mom except for attitude about their common situation—a kid who can't play ball well. The socialist mom, as mentioned, will drone on about the game of life, rules, fairness, etc, etc. The bench warmer's mom is a lot more open and direct about her feelings than this.

In her good moments, the bench warmer's mom is pretty humorous. She'll loudly question the parentage of the coach of the team, swear at umpires, and take umbrage at any remarks made by the parents of decent ballplayers. You can really get her stirred up by just pointing out gaffes that the coach's kid makes. I did hear a conversation one time between a bench warmer's mom and a coach that would have made a longshoreman blush. The whole deal revolved around the coach's kid making a gaffe at shortstop—the exact position the bench warmer's mom wanted her son to play.

BWM: "My son Brewster makes that play blindfolded. Course, he can't make it sitting on the damn bench while ol' Hands of Stone there plays."

Coach: "My son was an all-star in this league last year, ma'am."

BWM: "We all know that the all-star team is made up of coaches' and sponsors' kids. Don't give me that shit. You're afraid if my Brewster gets in the game that he's gonna show your little piddle-head up."

Coach: "Piddle-head? Now look here, you don't want me to tell you why I don't play your son."

BWM: "Tell me. I need a good laugh."

Coach: "I don't play him because he can't catch the ball and he spends half the time picking his nose out on the field. Snot lovers don't make good shortstops, not to mention the fact that he makes all the parents gag when he's in there."

BWM: "You have a lot of nerve. They say all men with small penises do."

I'm stopping here because I'm not sure I can spell some of the cuss words that were used beyond this point in the conversation. This tender discussion finally concluded when the BWM was asked by the umpire to leave the stands. Even while leaving she tossed one-liners out about the umpire's family difficulties. It seems that hell hath no fury like a Bench Warmer's Mother scorned.

For sheer daffiness, however, the following parental type takes the championship belt.

Type Five—Don't Understand the Game Mom

She's enough to make you chew up carpet. You can always depend on her to ask some lame-ass questions about the game at an extremely critical moment. It's like she's out there on Jupiter while the rest of us occupy good ol' terra firma. Witness this actual conversation . . .

(Game situation—bases are loaded, one out, our team is down by two runs. Bottom of the last inning).

DUGM: "Mighty cool breeze out tonight isn't it?"

MIS (man in stands): "Um . . . yeah."

DUGM: "Think I should've had my Ralphie wear a long sleeved t-shirt tonight."

(Strike one goes by. Count is O and one.)

MIS: "Dammit to hell. C'mon Freddie! We need this worse than Clinton needs alibis!"

DUGM: "That's funny. Why is the coach moving his hands all around like that? Is he sick or does he have muscular problems or something?"

(Strike two goes by. Count is O and two.)

MIS: "Damn, damn, damn! (looks over at DUGM) Do you have a clue as to what is happening here?"

(Ball one. Count is one and two.)

DUGM: "Why of course I do. It's windy and the boys are having a good time. What else do I need to know? And could you tell me if the coach is having a muscular problem?"

MIS: "Lady, this is a ballgame. The coach is using signals to message his players and tell them what to do."

(Ball two. Count is two and two.)

MIS: "Yes! Watch 'em close there, Freddie!"

DUGM: "Why doesn't he just yell out what he wants them to do?"

(Ball three. Count is full, three balls and two strikes.)

MIS: "Lady, if he yells out what he wants them to do the other team will get an unfair advantage. The signals keep the other team confused."

DUGM: "They're sure keeping me confused. Wonder why those boys wear gloves when they bat. Do you know?"

(Batter fouls off the next pitch. The count is still three and two.)

MIS: "Got a good hack at that one. You'll get hold of one, Freddie!"

DUGM: "The gloves aren't a gang thing, are they?"

(Next pitch catches the batter looking, outside corner strike. The game is over.)

MIS: "Dammit all to hell! And we would've gone to the playoffs if we'd won!"

DUGM: "Serves him right for being in a gang. It'll just lead him to prison."

The bad thing about this is that I could quote four to five more real conversations like this one without breaking a sweat. The ironic thing is, some of 'em come from ladies with kids who have played Little League ball for years. I can't imagine not picking up some knowledge about the game in this period of time, but the "don't understand the rules mom" continues to go to the games in a cloud of ignorance that even Tommy Lasorda couldn't help her overcome.

You will find that tolerance for the "don't understand the rules mom" is based upon what physical category she happens to fall into. If she is a haint mom, she will be derided and scorned for her lack of knowledge. If she's in our next category, the "centerfold mom," she will be seen as cute and adorable. This is true even though she typically has a baseball IQ somewhat less than a box of Rice Krispies.

Type Six—Centerfold Mom

This is my favorite stereotypical parental type. Ain't ashamed to admit it, either. Hell, I'm not dead yet, and the moment that a pretty woman doesn't brighten my day is the point in life I'll start buying Perry Como albums. I'm very proud to say that I just luv the centerfold mom.

God seems to have decreed that each baseball season I'll have one centerfold mom sitting there in the stands with me. This is as it should be. And the best thing about it is, I get to sit close to her while I watch all the games.

You may think that I'm being egotistical by saying I'll get to sit close to the centerfold mom. I'm not being egotistical at all—it's just the way it is. The bottom line is that I'm the senior member of the Brotherhood.

We attract women like magnets, despite the fact that all we do is treat them in a friendly, polite manner. It's just the way things are. Suffice it to say that you should just accept the fact that a centerfold mom will sit close to me as these games are being played. It's the way nature intended it.

Sitting with a centerfold mom enhances the overall game experience. The game seems to be more vivid, the sunshine brighter, the sounds more intense. To sit back and admire her beauty is a delightful pleasure. I find the best way to enjoy the game experience with her is to sit high up in the stands, at least two or three levels higher than where she is sitting. From this vantage point, you can not only see the game, but furtive glances downward can reveal pink topography much nicer than any of the mountain ranges you're aware of.

You do have to be careful when ogling the centerfold mom. The most obvious problem you'll be faced with is how to best disguise the ogling from your spouse. I've found the best way to do this is to position yourself so that your wife is to your left, and the centerfold mom is sitting about three or so rows down to your right. This works out well cause you can then appear to be looking straight ahead, yet, glancing downward and slightly to the right reveals the centerfold mom. The only thing about all this glancing back and forth is that it can give you a helluva headache. You also run the risk of her catchin' you lookin', but this is typically not a problem. The centerfold mom is accustomed to being stared at, and, in some cases, even appreciates it. I actually had one slip me a little wink one time as she caught me glancing at some of her more hormonally stimulatory body parts. She knows that she is a work of art, and accepts the stares with a grace and kindness second to none.

At some point during the season you'll imagine yourself whisking the centerfold mom off to an exotic location for lovemaking sessions equivalent to the uninhibited snake sex I'll describe for you in Chapter 9. The best thing to do when this happens is to forget any ideas about making these fantasies a reality—the centerfold mom is usually mated with a guy who would best be described as a well-developed ape with his hair partially removed. In addition, his tolerance for would-be wife fornicators tends to be zero. And look, I know it's terrible to talk about wanting to make love with someone else's wife, but the fact of the matter is all of us guys in the stands would give up a gonad to conjugate with the centerfold mom. And you women should allow us that mental pleasure. We know that we're never gonna get the chance to abuse her, anyway. The psuedo-Kong she's married to will see to it that it never happens.

Like a work of art, the centerfold mom can be summed up as a veritable cornucopia of aesthetic pleasures. A far contrast from the . . .

Type Seven—Solicitor Dad

God, if the word *nimrod* ever fit a human being it fits this guy. You know the type—he typically works for an insurance company, stock brokerage, or car dealership or might even sell Amway on the side. He's a real dick because he has one main problem—he can't stop selling. Even at the ballpark.

After a long day on the job you do look forward to a good ballgame. You know, the kind where you can just kick back, gaze at the field, smell the grass, and generally enjoy the pleasures of the game. These aesthetics are very hard to appreciate when you sit next to the solicitor dad. In fact, you don't know a game is going on when you sit next to him.

The solicitor dad will strike up a conversation with you at the drop of a hat. He's always got something he wants to sell and he ain't choosey about when he sells it. I actually think you could be taking a dump and the solicitor dad wouldn't care. He'd hold his nose and go for it. Actually, he might get a sale that way, too. I'd sure pay to have some privacy while dropping the cargo.

It's interesting when a game to gets underway to watch the migratory habits of the solicitor dad. He'll sit off to the side, supposedly to watch the game. What he's actually doing is sizing up the crowd, looking for his first mark of the evening. Typically, he will first hone in on another parental type that we haven't talked about, the pussy-whipped husband. When the solicitor dad notices how docile and agreeable this person is, he'll know that he'll be just as agreeable when he solicits him. And solicit him he will. Witness this actual conversation:

SD: "It's wonderful watching these children play ball, isn't it?"

PH: "Yes, it is. Makes a person glad to be alive."

SD: "It's a shame, though, that it is so hard to see the field. That sun is pretty fierce today."

PH: "Man, I'll say. My eyes are watering from the brightness and I forgot to bring my sunglasses."

SD: (homing in for the kill) "You're not still using regular sunglasses are you?"

PH: "Why, yes, I am. Are you telling me that there's something better?"

SD: "God, yes. Have you ever heard of Rayblockerz?"

PH: "No, I haven't. Should I have heard of them?"

SD: "Damn right you should. Best sunshades out on the market. They have a new technology that actually takes the sun's rays and deflects them into the ground. All you see is a cool, shaded scene. Very comforting and saves tons of wear and tear on the eyes!"

PH: "Damn—I sure wish I had a pair of 'em right now!"

SD: (somewhat like the shark in *Jaws*) "You can get a pair of 'em right now. I happen to own the middle-Georgia distributorship for Rayblockerz! I can go out to my car and get you a pair right now. The best thing is, I can sell 'em to you for an unheard of price—$21.99!"

PH: (knowing all eyes are on him and he doesn't want to appear cheap) "That's a wonderful price. Can I write you out a check?"

SD: "Sure can." (Gets up to go out to his car) "By the way, are you interested in losing some weight, too?"

You get the picture. If there are enough pussy-whipped husbands in the stands, the solicitor dad can make deals like this his full-time avocation. Fortunately, the pussy-whipped dad is not an overly abundant species (mortgaged my soul on that one, but we men do have to maintain some sense of pride), but his mere presence at the game is the fuel that drives the solicitor dad.

The best way of dealing with the solicitor dad? Try selling *him* something. I had one try to sell me a timeshare condo deal several years ago. I told him that I would be real glad to talk further with him about it if he'd be interested in looking at some good life insurance I happened to be selling. After that, the solicitor dad sorta tensed up and told me he had to go put some salve on some poison oak rashes he had. He then left the stands in a full-fledged trot towards his car.

I guess, when you get right down to it, that these Little League parental types are the main categories of nimrods the parents of good Little League players have to deal with. And they're everywhere Little League ball happens to be played, regardless of what part of the country you happen to live or work in. I guess they're just one part of the Little League experience that one has to accept and get accustomed to. Just remember that these people can be dealt with successfully. Don't think so? Think of it like this, then—if you can deal with TV evangelists, politicians, yankees, in-laws, dentists (excepting Dr. Boland, who is the Elvis of dentists), cranky babies, and your boss, you can damn well deal with these people. And you'll do it. I have faith in you. Why? Because I know you're a pussy-whipped husband like I am, and when your wife tells you to deal with them, you'll do it. It's as simple as that.

Chapter 9
ODDS, SODS, AND CLODS

☾

When you raid the whorehouse,
you take the piano player wit'cha!
— Ed Sr.

Since I began writing, I"ll go through periods where it's hard for me to come up with anything to write about. Then, I'll hit times when I can come up with all sorts of ideas. Many of these times, the ideas are not enough, in and of themselves, to create chapters, but are still things I'd like to write about. So I'm going to cover these things here. You may as well read it as you have already bought (I hope), borrowed (you cheap shit), or checked out (real cheap shit) this book.

People who ride bicycles on highways or streets must harbor a death wish

Think about it—have you ever been driving on a highway or busy street when a bike rider approaches you? It always happens to me when there is traffic on both sides of the road. The bicycler approaches, giving off the air that he owns the road and that you'd better move. And you can't! Two thoughts consistently come to mind when this situation presents itself. First, how much intelligence does it take for a bike rider to challenge thousands of pounds of motorized metal? And second, it's always a man who does this. Women are different, as the outfits they wear when bicycling are enough to cause me to immediately forgive them for being on my side of the road.

I harbor a secret wish when a bike rider approaches me. I always wish I could somehow scare the hell out of them but not really hurt them. Just scare them enough so they'll use common sense and ride their bikes on quiet streets, or in the country, or whatever. And don't give me a bunch of crap about how they are saving fossil fuels. Whatever fuel they save is offset by the driver's eyestrain factor. What I mean by this is, when you approach these bike riders in the open daylight, the glare that comes off their pale white legs is very damaging to the eyes. We could save tens of thousands of dollars in annual eye exam costs for drivers by just getting these kamikaze bikers off our roads and highways.

In the past, Hugh has made the comment that real men don't ride bikes anyway. Really, they can't. Ever check out today's bike seat design? It really crowds out the pink crusader and gonads. I'm not just going on Hugh's word, though (even though, as a member of the Brotherhood, his word is gospel). I researched this topic myself. A kid who lives down the street from us bought his new racing bike over for Alison to take a look at (she's fifteen now and draws boys like flies). As he paraded the bike around, I thought, what the hell, and asked the kid if I could take a quick ride? As he was on my property, there was only one answer he could give. He handed the bike over.

I walked up, grabbed it, and looked at the seat—it appeared to be little more than a solid chunk of hard black rubber. I thought it looked uncomfortable as hell, but, I was thinking that maybe I didn't understand it and that today's technology would insure that the seat would be comfortable.

Wrong! I got up on that thing and slowly sat down. I could then feel the crusader and his friends being mashed up into my body. Since I have no inherent desire to pulverize my gonads, I got off the bike and made some lame excuse about a pulled muscle. It was all I could do. Ed Jr. told me a long time ago that it was a piss-poor man that doesn't protect his cardsack.

So, bike riders, take heed to these remarks. There are lots of folks who, down deep, feel exactly like I do. We just don't go around talking about it because it sounds like you're being a foe of the environment or something. That's not it at all—I simply despise being placed in a situation where my choices are to either wreck ol' Black (my '92 Toyota pick-up, which I love more than life itself), or to nail the hell out of a bike rider. That's no choice at all. Bike riders, think hard about it and take up the sport of alligator wrestling instead. It'll satisfy your penchant for early death, and your odds are better with the gator.

Shemp was the funniest of the Three Stooges

Now, I know this statement is gonna create a lot of controversy. Many Stooge fans liked Curly, or Larry, or even Moe the best. But there is no doubt in my mind that Shemp was the funniest Stooge of them all. His long, scraggly, greasy hair, his bulbous nose, and all those crazy sounds he made—without doubt, those attributes made Shemp the true Grand Master of Comedy. Hugh and Ray totally agree with me on this, so nothing else needs be said.

Mother Luck can be a fickle mistress

Several years ago, before they voted in the Georgia lottery, Ed Jr. got into a deal where he played the Canadian lottery every week. The way he played was, they mailed him the slips, he marked his numbers on them, and then sent them in. The game he was playing was one where you picked five numbers and, if you matched them exactly, you could win hundreds of thousands of dollars.

I learned about all these nuances of the Canadian lottery during one of my Juliette visits with Ed Jr. As he rattled off how he'd gotten into this scheme, I laughed and told him that all he was gonna do was give his money to the Canadians. Of course, he gave me one of his looks that indicated a real questioning of my parentage, and told me that no one ever did anything worthwhile without taking a chance. Then, he went on about explaining the game to me.

One evening, a month or so after this conversation, he called me. Soon as I picked up the phone I heard, "Damn Mother Luck!"

"Dad, is that you?" I asked.

"Hell, yes, it's me," Ed Jr. tenderly stated.

"Who in the hell is Mother Luck?"

He didn't answer this question, but launched right into telling me how he had matched four of the five numbers on the last Canadian lottery drawing. My heart sank a little when I realized that he was just one number away from winning the entire jackpot. I then asked him a question that, in retrospect, I wished I hadn't asked.

"How far off were you on the number you missed?"

"I picked thirty-three and the number was thirty-four."

I was silent just from the implication—one number away from riches. I then asked another question I probably shouldn't have.

"What would you have won if you'd gotten the number right?"

"Seven hundred and fifty thousand dollars," he replied.

Three-quarters of a million dollars—and just one number off! As the sheer magnitude of what had happened registered in my mind, Ed Jr. summed it up pretty thoroughly with this statement, "Yeah, Mother Luck moved her lips and stuck her ass right in my face."

And there you have it. Mother Luck had proven herself to be a fickle mistress to Ed Jr. But take heart in the fact that at least you now know who Mother Luck is—the patron saint of all lottery players, as defined by Ed Jr. I'd give you more information about Mother Luck, but, when I mentioned her a few weeks ago in a conversation with my dad, he cussed as badly as the time Preacher Garrett tried to visit us on Super Bowl Sunday. Ed Jr. and Mother Luck are in an estranged relationship right now. Let's just leave it at that.

Snake sex

Sometimes you go through life and get to thinking that you've seen almost everything there is to see, and done most everything there is to do. That's not how it is at all, though. People learn new things every day. I sure do.

Just last week I was flipping through channels on the TV and came across a nature documentary. This one, though, was a little bit different than most because the first footage I noticed was that of two horses making love. I have to admit it sort of put me in shock because it's not the typical thing you see on TV—prime-time horse porno. I do have to admit it was sort of interesting watching them, but the main thing I got out of it was a huge sense of awe regarding the dimensions of the male horse's anaconda of love.

Ray and Hugh told me I shouldn't admit to looking at it, but how could you not look? It was almost the size of a baseball bat, and I can remember thinking, "If I had that, I wouldn't have to work for a living anymore."

As the show progressed, it became apparent that it was showcasing the lovemaking habits of animals. Most of it was pretty nondescript except for a couple of species. Lizards were the most fun to watch. The male gets on top of the female and humps her brains out. It almost reminded me of the Brotherhood's daily routine during our college days. Lizards are uninhibited, for sure, and get their money's worth out of a sexual encounter.

After lizards, snakes commanded my attention. I have to be honest here—I hate a damn snake. Don't get me wrong, I know there are good ones, and people don't really understand them, but I'd rather sniff the seats at a Mexican restaurant than get near one. I just can't stand them, and I figure the deader they are, the better.

But snakes sure have interesting sex. As the show went on, the narrator was out strolling around in some grassy fields when, suddenly, he got very still. I wondered why he was so quiet until the camera panned the ground.

There they were—two large, black snakes. I think they were some kind of rat snakes or something. Anyway, they appeared to be around three feet each in length, and were rolling around on the ground like crazy.

I honestly thought they'd lucked up on a snake fight—two large, black snakes fighting it out to the death. The people producing this show cleared that misconception up quickly, though. These snakes weren't fighting; they were mating. I could tell this clearly enough when the camera panned in close. There, right before my eyes, was this tiny pink snake dick. I kid you not! It looked just like a guy's (circumcised, no less), and the male was using it in such a way that I thought he was a Williams. He was definitely givin' his little reptilian gonads a major workout.

I sat there and noticed that snakes do have a couple of advantages that we humans don't. As they frolicked around I noticed that their facial expressions never changed. I know snakes don't typically change facial expressions, but this was one time where I thought you might see them crook their mouths up into a little smile or something. No such luck—their expressions never changed. That could be either good or bad, depending upon the perspective of the snake. The good side of it would be if you were a male snake only interested in your own gratification you wouldn't really know if you were making love properly or poorly. No facial expressions means no one knows how it's going and, therefore, neither party has to really care. Just get the job done and move on.

The second advantage snakes have is, because they make no noise, snakes can make love often because there is less chance of them getting caught at it. That's where we people screw up. I can think of more than one time in my life where I wanted to make love with someone but couldn't because people were close by. That's what always stopped matters from proceeding—the woman would always be afraid that someone "will hear us." If people were quiet like snakes, we could just mute out when having sex and then be able to accomplish the act in elevators, movie theatres, or wherever else we wanted to do it.

So, I'll sum this segment up by stating that I do hate snakes but snake sex is pretty damn interesting. Before closing, I do need to thank my snake sex technical advisor, Linda Bleser. Linda is a good writing friend of mine and seems to have a handle on this snake sex business. She has enlightened me to lots of its nuances, dispensing wisdom on items as diverse as like snake foreplay or egg-laying habits. Linda is not an animal authority but she seems to know about these snakes; therefore, any technical questions I referred to her regarding their breeding habits were always very professionally answered. Linda, many thanks, and yer the best, you know.

Bad gas pains when you're in the car with your date

There's not a man alive this hasn't happened to. You're in your car with a date, the windows are up, and that bean burrito casserole you had for lunch is creating some urgent pressures in your lower abdominal regions. You have to do something, but traditionally the choices were as follows:

1. Pinch it back, and risk the implosion of your intestinal tract.

2. Release the vile vapors, pray that the emission is silent, and have the odor inside your car resemble that of an expired frog.

3. Release the vile vapors with a noisy emission. Unless you have a dog in the back seat, or you're the kind who's prideless and blames your date, you can consider your relationship with her finished if this happens. Forever. And then hope that she doesn't go tell her friends about what happened.

Big Al, whom I mentioned in the first book and who shit in his pants during a final, never lived it down. He couldn't have gotten a date after that if he'd paid someone to go out with him. The bottom line is—if you fart loudly with a woman in your car she will never go out with you again. She may tell others about it, too. Always remember that.

This happened to a couple of friends of mine. In both cases, they paid dearly for their misfortune. Fortunately, this fate doesn't have to befall you, for the master of dating psychology, Ed Jr., figured out a solution for this particular problem a long time ago.

If I remember it right, I told Ed Jr. years ago about a buddy of mine who had this unfortunate experience during a date. We both laughed like hell about what happened—it seems that a buddy of mine named Fred decided to take this girl into Forsyth one night for some fast food. While driving there, Fred slipped and farted out loud. After the fart, Fred said that his date demanded that he pull the car over. He did, and his date staggered out and began coughing a lot. He tried to go over and console her, but she told him to get his unmannered ass out of her field of vision. After a few minutes of hacking, she informed Fred that he was going to drive her to a pay phone. Fred was bewildered at her request but did as she asked. When they got to a pay phone she put the money in, called her parents, and told them that they needed them to pick her up immediately. Fred said that he had never been more embarrassed in his life. He begged her to get back in the car. She quickly advised him that she'd take a bath in acid before she'd get back into "that dank pit." Fred then had to stand by and wait for her parents to arrive and get her. They did finally pull up, got out, and asked their daughter what had happened? She told them Fred had farted out loud in the car and advised them that he was a "gas-spurting maniac." Her parents looked at Fred like he was some kind of rogue skunk, and then gave him a speech about self-pride and personal dignity. After that, they hustled her into the car and left Fred alone to ponder these tender events.

Ed Jr. laughed like hell at this but said that it was all unnecessary. When I asked him what he meant by that, he said, "There's no reason why a man can't relieve gas pains and still have a good time on a date. Let me tell you how to do it."

He did, and his plan made sense. So much sense, in fact, that I put it into action one evening when I was taking a date to Macon. Earlier that particular day, my brother and I had to go to Forsyth to run some errands for my mom. While in Forsyth, we snuck over to the Nu-Way and I had a big lunch—six chili dogs, if I remember correctly. We both did our business in town and got back to Juliette that afternoon.

I guess as I drove my date (I think it was Jenny) to Macon that evening that those six chili dogs decided it was time to send me a message—and boy, did they. My stomach began cramping like crazy, and I could tell that I might be about to have some problems.

My first obvious symptom of distress was the feeling that my gut was rapidly becoming a Goodyear blimp. It seemed to be swelling up and taking on some kind of mutant life form of its own. Attempting to alleviate the rapidly building pressures, I shifted positions in my car seat a few times, thinking (hoping) that it would do some good. It didn't help, though. I continued to feel more and more miserable. I decided I could just tough it out and this stratagem actually worked for a few minutes. After that, a sharp pain that I felt all over told me that the zero hour was near.

You know what the zero hour is. That moment when there is no doubt as to the immediate need to fart. It's like when you have to sneeze—you can think about not sneezing, but you will. It's inevitable. And it's the same way with farts. You have to do it—no ifs, ands, or buts about it.

I knew that I had about twenty seconds in which to release the pressure. I also knew that after all those chili dogs that breaking wind in the car would make the upholstery smell like a ditch digger's t-shirt. It was time to put Ed Jr.'s well-thought out plan into action.

I looked over at Jenny and told her that the rear end of the car seemed to be vibrating. She asked me if I knew what was causing it. I told her I didn't have a clue, but felt that it had better be checked out. After I said this, I pulled the car over on the side of the road.

Jenny looked a little concerned, but I told her that I just wanted to get out and check the rear end to be absolutely sure nothing was wrong. I also shot her a line about being concerned about her safety and all. Then, I reached up, flicked on the radio, and told her it would keep her company while I got out and checked out the car.

I left the car running, pulled up the emergency brake, and got out. Quickly, I slammed the door shut, and ran around to the back of the car. Jenny turned around and looked at me through the glass. I gave her an assuring smile, then got a concerned expression on my face, and kneeled down as if to check the tires or trunk of the car.

"BRAP!" It sounded like a large bullfrog announcing his presence. Basically, I felt like I'd dropped five pounds when I broke this major wind. A couple of more modest blasts followed. Then, I quickly got up, ran to the car, got in, and slammed the door.

You have to do this because it's a well-known fact that major farts seem to follow a person. I really mean it. If I hadn't run, jumped in, and shut the door quickly, I would have pulled the whole fart back inside the car with me. This is a scientific fact. If you don't believe this, check with Ed Jr. He'll confirm it for you.

As I pulled back out on the highway, Jenny asked me if I'd found the problem and fixed it. I told her, with a very straight face, that I had. And it was true—I had fixed it. I then told her a little white lie about the difficulty being a large rock stuck in the tread on one of the rear tires. Okay, I know that's a bald-faced lie, but isn't it better than telling her I'd eaten six chili dogs and was fartin' like a sailor? Sometimes you have to use basic common sense and go with your instincts. If everyone told the truth all the time, there would be no lawyers or politicians around. I'm pretty sure I did the right thing.

So go with this strategy if major gas pains interrupt what should be a pleasurable dating experience. And don't let it bother you if a carload of your buddies happens by, catches you squatting behind your car, and begins laughing like hell. They'll know what you're up to. But who cares—better them than your date, right? Only you know best how to deal with your own personal methane supply.

To piss or not to piss—that is the question

Until I became a teenager, I'd never even heard of the shy bladder syndrome. I'm sure most of y'all know what it is—it's a problem that doesn't get a lot of press, but it's out there. Basically, those afflicted can't take their pinksters out and piss in front of other people (usually other guys—men don't typically piss in front of women unless it's a desperation situation). You see it a lot at ballgames. Men have to piss in those long, trough-looking things, and at times sixty or seventy can be squeezed in there together. The shy bladder sufferer has to wait for a stall to open up, as the troughs are a no man's land for the man who has a reluctant bladder. I hate to admit this, but most men who have to piss badly seem to have no compassion for a man who can't.

Years ago in Juliette, way back in the thirties or forties, the shy bladder issue was firmly dealt with. At that time, semipro baseball games were occasionally played in the community. These games typically drew good crowds as there were locals on some of the teams, plus the level of play was excellent. Ed Jr. told me that several hundred people typically went to the ballpark on any given night, and these crowds hollered, cussed, and really enjoyed themselves at the ballpark.

On the night here in question, Homer Chambliss was one of the spectators in the stands. (Y'all remember Homer from the first book— he ran the general store down the street from Ed Sr.). Homer was a real good man. He would give you the shirt off his back, and was known as a straight shooter. If you got into a conversation with him regarding any subject, he would give you his opinion directly and with lots of conviction. His voice carried a long ways, so if Homer happened to express himself, anyone within a half mile radius knew the point he was trying to make.

Ed Jr. said that on this particular night he noticed Homer moving back and forth between the ballgame and his car. He said that he didn't directly see anything, but assumed Homer was going out, having a little nip, and then returning to the ballpark.

Several innings of the game went by, and Homer began feeling the need to siphon his trouser snake. As the need got more urgent he got up and walked out of the stands onto a side field that adjoined the ballpark.

The reason Homer went to this side field is that the only bathroom facility available to the crowd was located there. It was just a privy—a little wooden shack with a hand lettered sign on it that read "Outhouse."

Outhouse or not, Homer had to piss, and as soon as possible. As he walked up and got in line, he noticed that there were at least twenty people in front of him. He knew that he'd have to wait "almost till I was on Medicaid" to shake the dew off his lily. There was no choice, though. He had to stand in line and wait.

Homer said the wait was so long that he was beginning to cross his legs and do involuntary drag queen impersonations. It didn't help matters any that a small kid in line just in front of him had an accident while doing his duty inside the outhouse. Apparently, this kid had been eating green plums and his intestinal tract suddenly decided to teach him a lesson. As Homer delicately put it, "That kid shit all over himself. If he'd gotten any more on him, he would've had to have wiper blades put on his glasses so that he could see."

Homer said the kid's parents were frantically running around, trying to find some old clothes for him to wear home. The search got so long and drawn out that Homer finally stripped off his shirt, walked up to the kid's parents, and said, "Let his stinky little ass wear that."

The kid's father looked like he was pissed off due to Homer's comment, but the mother was grateful, even though Homer had been less than genteel towards their child. I guess when your kid is covered in crap you're desperate for any help that's offered. Regardless of what they felt, they cleaned up their kid as best they could, and threw Homer's shirt over him. Then, they hustled him off towards their car, and a fetid trip home.

Once these human turtles had left the line, it began moving a lot more quickly. More quickly, that is, until the person in front of Homer stepped up to bat in the privy.

The guy in line in front of Homer was Junior Jackson. Junior was a good ol' boy who drove a pulpwood truck for a living. He was a real big man, too—probably close to six-foot-five, and weighed right around three hundred pounds. He was a hard worker, loved a good ballgame, and could burp louder than any human being I have ever heard in my life. I swear that when he clutched out a belch you honestly thought there was a chance he was expelling about half his internal organs. It was that loud. It honestly sounded like his diaphragm was vibrating when he cut one loose.

Before this particular night, everyone in Juliette thought they knew all there was to know about Junior. But there was one thing no one knew—Junior had a bad case of the shy bladder syndrome.

In plain English, Junior couldn't take a piss with anyone watching him. And, as everyone in line found out that night, he couldn't take one with people waiting on him, either. As Junior closed the privy door, I'm sure everyone in line (especially Homer) felt that he would be in there maybe one to two minutes. This didn't turn out to be the case. As everyone patiently stood in line, a minute passed, then two, then three. Before long, several more minutes had passed, and the line had grown by an additional fifteen to twenty people.

Homer must've been frustrated as hell at this point. It had to be like getting to the pearly gates and suddenly finding the door slammed shut on you. I can only imagine Homer standing there in line, impatiently rocking back and forth with a toothpick in his mouth. I'll bet that his face was redder than a tomato fertilized with badger balls.

Soon, ten-plus minutes had passed. Ed Jr. said at this point the line had to be up to around thirty or more people. At the literal end of his rope, Homer decided that it was now time to take action. Walking right up to the privy door, he shouted, "If you can't piss, step aside and let a man that can!"

Ed Jr. said that it got quiet for a second, and then everyone started laughing. Laughing hard. So hard that one guy had to excuse himself and run in the woods.

After Homer's comment, Junior stumbled out of the privy, his face redder than a redbug with blisters. Looking at the gathered crowd, he shouted, "Just how can a man piss with all this racket?"

Homer immediately replied, "Like this." He then proceeded to reach in his britches, withdraw nature's fire hydrant, and unleashed a yellow geyser of piss right out in front of the crowd!

Ed Jr. said that if people laughed when Homer first hollered at Junior, they went into overdrive over this turn of events. Junior got even redder in the face and stalked off fuming into the darkness. His ass had been whupped, and he knew it. Homer calmly stood there with all those folks watching him, finished draining his lizard, and then calmly zipped it back up. As he walked away, he looked at all the assembled crowd, and stated, "Always back it up if yer right about something."

And there you have it—the correct way of dealing with people who suffer from the shy bladder syndrome. I'll bet Junior never again held up a line of people after this episode. In fact, Ed Jr. said that he didn't think Junior attended another ballgame for the next several years after this incident. And that's as it should be. No point in him going, not being able to piss, and holding up people who could.

As for Homer, he attended many more ballgames over the years. A funny thing happened at those games, too. Ed Jr. said after this incident people would step aside if Homer got in line, and would immediately let him move to the front of said line. If you think about it a second, it was a pretty smart thing to do. Would you like to chance being the person in line in front of Homer? I wouldn't, 'cause I learned that sometimes in life, you've gotta step aside and "let a man that can."

Buckshottin' frogs in Jones County

For those of you not in the know, Jones County adjoins Monroe County, (the county that contains the big city of Juliette) in my neck of the woods here in Georgia. I have many friends who live over in Jones County, not the least of whom is my Sunday School teacher,

Dale Washburn. Dale is a great guy. He's an excellent Sunday school teacher, and a good realtor to boot. In fact, Dale specializes in selling Jones County real estate. I'm very sure Dale could tell you some of the same kind of stories about events in Jones County that I've written about here in Monroe County. He's well-known there, respected, and I'll also mention that Dale is a devoted husband and the father of four children.

Those are the characteristics of Dale Washburn that everyone knows and respects. But, and I hate to bring this out into the open, there is a much darker side to Dale. A much, much darker side. A side that, to this point, he has kept very carefully hidden from the general public.

Dale Washburn is a frog abuser. That's right, a frog abuser. The bad thing about it is that he readily admits to it. Of course, most psychologists say that the first step towards recovery from a problem begins when the afflicted person admits having it. Dale does admit to frog abuse in his past. We can at least credit him with being honest about it. It still doesn't make his unholy cravings any easier to stomach, though. But his story can now be told, the true story of Dale Washburn, abuser of frogs.

It seems that rural Jones County in the fifties and sixties was not a real swinging place to grow up. There were few, if any, outlets for entertainment. There were no movie theatres, bowling alleys, or anything else that might be a way for kids to have fun. Oh sure, there was a pool hall and a bowling alley, but decent kids weren't allowed by their parents to patronize them. So, bottom line, there wasn't very much for a kid to do.

What was a young Jones Countian supposed to do without credible entertainment choices? Well, I guess most kids there did like I did—they created their own entertainment by using their wits. It's really not that hard to do if you use some imagination and creativity.

You can get on an old tire swing, hold a water balloon in your hand, and become an Air Force fighter pilot, strafing the Iraqi countryside. Walking across some old logs can make you the high-wire acrobat at the circus. Floating around in a pond converts you into an Olympic-class swimmer. Ultimately, and I hope you get the essence of what I'm talking about here, a rural child's imagination and creativity could take him into many new worlds. It could stimulate his imagination, and help him occupy otherwise dead time. But, some of us went a little further with our imagination than did others. Some of us pushed the envelope a bit too far.

Some of us like Dale Washburn. Dale got to the creativity fork in the road and took the less traveled path. Dale took the road that leads to blatant frog abuse.

It all started innocently enough. Dale was out on his back porch one morning watching some wasps hover about a new nest they were building. It was pretty hot, and the day looked like it was gonna be another long, boring one.

Upon noticing movement in his backyard, Dale stepped up to his back porch door to investigate. Upon opening the door, he saw a large bullfrog hopping around in the back yard. According to Dale, he was a damn big frog, too, "almost as big as a brand new softball."

Dale walked out and stalked the frog for lack of anything else better to do. At first, he was just gonna follow it around, but he decided to pick it up and carry it on the porch. At least with the frog on the porch, Dale would have a little company, even if that company was green and slimy. Dale said the frog was easy to catch because of its size, but when nabbed he pissed all over Dale's hand with a "stream big as the Ocmulgee River."

Dale took the frog inside and put it down on the porch floor. For the first few minutes the frog just sat still, no doubt assessing its new digs. After about ten minutes or so of this, the frog began hopping around. Dale said that it was fun to watch him do this at first, but after awhile he stopped watching the frog and began reading a book.

While reading the book, Dale began to get sleepy and eventually nodded off. A quick movement in the room caused him to awaken, though. As he opened his eyes, he saw the frog snap up a fly that had been buzzing around his porch all morning.

What caught Dale's attention the most was the fact that the frog had snapped up the fly in mid-air with his tongue. As Dale put it, "Its tongue ran out there like a whip, snapped up the fly, and sucked it down faster than a you can eat a Nu-Way hotdog. Then I noticed it looking around for more food to eat."

Because of the size of the fly and its dark color, Dale began wondering if the frog could be fooled into eating something that looked like a fly. Noting a box of shotgun shells sticking out of the pocket of his dad's jacket (which was hung up on a rack on the corner of the porch), he reached in and extracted one shell. Bursting the shell casing open, he filled his hands with the buckshot inside.

Dale looked at one of these pellets and decided he would see if the frog would eat one. He got a handful of the buckshot, walked over, and sat down within a few feet of the frog.

According to Dale, the frog just sort of sat there, stoically looking at him. When Dale was sure he had the frog's undivided attention, he took one of the tiny, dark pellets and rolled it across the floor towards it.

"SNAP" went the frogs tongue! It sucked up the buckshot faster than a politician takes a personal check. In fact, within seconds, it was again looking stoically at Dale and waiting to see if he was going to feed it again.

Now, at this point, most individuals of moderation would have had their laughs and gone on about their business. But not Dale—Dale decides that if the frog's eating one piece of buckshot was funny, two would be even funnier. Proceeding with this assumption, he rolls the second buckshot pellet towards the frog.

"SNAP!" The frog's tongue darted out quickly and with such focus that even Dale was taken aback. Dale said that he remembered thinking, "If I could get my tongue to move like that, I'd have a pretty damn interesting life." For decorum's sake, let's not even try to speculate on just what he meant by that.

Once Dale began rolling these pellets, he wouldn't stop. He fed pellets to that frog until he had literally rolled hundreds into it. After rolling them for several hours, Dale tired of his sadism and went outside to play and perhaps torture more innocent creatures.

When evening drew near, Dale re-entered the back porch area of his house. As he stood and looked around, it hit him that he had not let the frog go back outside after rolling all those pellets into it. He looked around for the frog, fearing that he might have found his way into the house. He knew if that happened, and his mom or dad found the frog, that he could expect his heiny to be turned redder than a whore's lipstick.

This fear soon became unfounded as Dale found the frog in the exact same spot he had left it in earlier in the day. As Dale walked over to the frog, it did not move and hop away as a frog normally would. Its problem, as Dale soon discovered, was that this frog couldn't hop away. It was so weighted down with buckshot pellets that he couldn't move an inch.

At first, Dale got a big laugh out of the frog's predicament. Then, it hit him that if the frog were left sitting on the porch, and his parents saw it full of buckshot, maybe his ass and hamburger meat were going to begin having a lot of similarities.

During times of duress you find out what kind of character a man has. Do you do the right thing, or not? Do you shade the truth, or not? Honestly, I can say little here, as my flight away from Jenny's house after I hit her dog showed me to have the character of a Yellow Pages lawyer. But, my character is not at issue here—Dale's is. (That's one of the good things about writing. You can take things in any direction you want them to go). I'm sure the tension is really starting to build with everyone now. Just exactly what did Dale do in this situation?

First, he realized he needed to get the heavy-leaded frog out of his parents' house, and quickly. As Dale astutely mentioned to me, "I had to get it off our property, fast. Think about it. What would Daddy have done if he'd seen me with that frog, stopped me, and then grabbed it away from me? That damn frog was slippery and wet. If Daddy grabbed it and it slipped out of his hands, he could have broken his foot or something."

I guess my mind is just not agile enough to think of possibilities like that. Anyway, Dale proceeded to run into the woods to find some place to deposit the frog. He looked in a variety of spots, trying to find the right resting place for his semimetallic toad. At first, he considered laying it up on a tree limb as he feared a predator would kill the immobilized frog if placed on the ground. Then, he figured that a frog on a limb might attract the attention of passers-by in the woods and could get bothered or hurt by them. Fearing that, the tree limb idea was quickly scratched.

The next thought Dale had was that he could place the frog in a grassy field. The green grass would camouflage the frog, and it could have time to expel the buckshot from its system and then hop away. Dale had to shelve this idea too. The hot Georgia sun could roast a leaden frog, and the fire ants would have a field day with it.

At this point, Dale began to realize that he had a real dilemma on his hands. He was just beginning to come up with another idea when he heard a loud voice wafting through the trees.

"Dale!"

It was Dale's dad! And it was suppertime! And at the Washburn household, you didn't dare come to the dinner table late. Why, you ask? First, it showed Dale's mother less than full respect for her efforts in preparing the meal. In the South, we honor our mothers in subtle ways. Being on time to eat is one of them. Second, Dale has several brothers and sisters. If you were a few minutes late getting to dinner it could mean sitting down to a table that looked like goats had attacked it— only leftovers available for you to eat. On rural Georgia tables in this era, leftovers for young boys were mostly things like beets, salmon croquets, or cabbage casseroles. Not the kind of stuff you wanted to sustain yourself with, for sure. Dale knew that if he didn't get moving towards that supper table that his stomach was gonna hate him like a 'possum hates the daylight.

As mentioned, I've found on numerous occasions during my lifetime that we discover, during times of trial, just what a man is made of. We'll see what kind of decisions he makes, which roads he'll travel, and what things he'll do or not do. Ultimately, we discover just what is inside the man.

This was a defining moment of truth for Dale when he heard his dad calling him. For at that instant, he was in a high pressure situation—be late for dinner and deal with the frog properly or neglect the frog, expose it to harm, but be on time for dinner. Which path forward would he chose?

Dale told me that he gave his quandary about five good seconds of intense thought. He then said, "I put an entire afternoon into messing around with that frog, and it was time for dinner. My stomach was emptier than a whore's promise. 'Sides, no matter what I did, something was gonna get that frog. Might be fire ants, might be a snake, or whatever. A fifty-pound frog is not very agile, you know. It was then that I realized what I had to do."

Dale picked up the frog and began running towards a nearby pond. What he intended to do was put the frog in a shallow part of the pond. By doing this, he figured, the frog would stay wet, fire ants wouldn't get it, it could nab a fly or two for dinner, and ultimately could sit there unbothered until it crapped out all those pellets.

This wasn't a bad plan, but what Dale didn't count on was the large water moccasin that slithered out of the bushes just as he got to the edge of the pond. When that snake crawled out, Dale screamed and flung his arms out in opposite directions—the net effect of this being that Fred Frog was shot putted into the air and launched directly into the water.

At first, Dale appreciated the distance he had gotten from throwing the frog, "a good fifteen feet, at least." He then said that the frog made a helluva splash as it hit the pond's surface. Shaking off these rather telling thoughts, Dale then realized what he had just done. He quickly decided that he would go into the water and try and save Fred's life. It was a noble thought, but then "DALE!"

It was Dale's dad, hollering for him to come to supper yet again. Dale realized what this holler meant by its tone. It meant that if he wasn't at the table in about one minute that his future spelled "a-s-s-w-h-u-p-p-i-n'." And not a casual ass-whuppin', either—a major one. Not coming to dinner when one's parents called was one of the most unforgivable sins that one could visit upon oneself or herself.

I'll bet most of you think that Dale did the right thing here. He waded out in the water, saved Fred Frog, and took an ass-whuppin' to save his slimy, green friend. WRONG! Dale said that the trade-off between a heavy frog and a throbbing ass was an easy one to make. He would give up the frog, enjoy a good meal, and save precious miles on his yet unblemished heinie.

I would've thought Dale might have had a hard time eating after abandoning his frog to that great lily pad in the sky, but this proved not to be the case. By all accounts, Dale ate like a visiting preacher, piling his plate high with goodies, and washing it all down with tall glasses of iced tea. After eating two whole plates of food, he even had room for several desert helpings. When his dinner was completed, he went out on the back porch, got in the swing, and relaxed and let his dinner settle.

Behavior like this is not totally unusual. Psychological case studies show that many murderers can calmly eat meals after they have performed the most heinous crimes imaginable. Such was the case with Dale, I guess. Whatever the circumstances, Fred Frog died an ignoble death that evening. History had forgotten him until this story.

So there you have it. The sad, touching death of Fred, a Jones County frog. A frog cursed because of his having had the misfortune of encountering Dale Washburn, a major abuser of said frogs. Maybe stuff like this is why Dale is such a good Sunday school teacher today. He engaged in awful sins like these and can show us the straight and right path by reflecting on his own wretched example. Just do me one favor—if you happen to meet Dale, don't mutter *ribbet*. If you do, you just might find some buckshot pellets zooming towards your opened mouth.

A major pet peeve

I hate to admit this about myself, and I'm not proud of it at all, but old people driving on the highways just about makes me crazy! God, I feel better just by owning up to it.

Look, I know I'm not that far away from getting old myself. I also have many good friends who are getting on up there in years. All that is well and good, but there's one thing I can count on every time I'm going down an interstate highway. If I happen to be on one and come upon someone doing twenty miles per hour in a seventy mile per hour zone, it will always be an old person. Always! I just don't understand what happens to us in our senior years that causes us to drive like turtles. I'll even bet that the slow driving causes accidents of all sorts—impatient hotheads like me try to get around the sluggish cars and then create all sorts of mayhem. Maybe this is how it's intended to be—the hotheaded driver and the elderly driver sort of negate each other's flaws with their driving habits. The elderly driver causes the hotheaded driver to slow down. Or the hotheaded driver causes the elderly driver to use more gasoline. I'm sure that's the answer! Hey, sometimes when you write, you can have the most eye-opening revelations! I've figured this whole thing out by just writing about it.

Pet Assassins

I know I'm gonna catch hell about this one. After reading this though, you'll have to admit that the thought is somewhat intriguing and could prove quite profitable for the shady yet success-driven entrepreneurial type.

Ponder this, if you will. How many times in the past have you been woken up by a dog who is yapping its ass off late at night? Or better yet, think about the stray cat who decided to meander in and drop a load of piss right into one of the insulated pockets in your new hunting jacket. And that said pocket held it because it was rain-proofed? And that you discovered it when you put your jacket on and plunged your hands into the pockets?

All of these things have happened to me. And I could toss even more examples in—a goose that decided it liked eating scraps out of our trash cans and then consistently left long lines of turds voluminous enough to have been used in making life-sized space shuttle replicas. Or the collie puppy that hacked like Velma (this was the first, and last, time Ed Jr. ever allowed a pet inside our house), with lungs that reverberated like bass drums.

When you sum it all up and really think about it, pets can be a major bother. No one wants to admit this out loud, but it's true. Political correctness just doesn't allow us to say it. The bottom line, though, is that pets do have a value; but when their mishaps exceed their worth, it's time to reconsider the decision to keep the pet.

It makes perfect sense. Why do people spend four hundred dollars for a veterinarian to stitch up a wound on Barfy the puppy when they can buy a brand new Barfy for fifty dollars? If you work the math, you could have eight new Barfys for the same price that it takes to get the original one reworked. And eight new Barfys, bought over a period of time, would give much more pleasure over many more years than the original Barfy would. It makes perfect, logical sense.

The reason people let themselves get screwed in this pet business is that they allow themselves to get too emotionally attached to their animals. There's nothing wrong in caring about your pet. The only thing is, when you assign the same value to an animal life as a human one, then you're asking for trouble. That's why a perfectly logical adult will spend a thousand dollars to fix Tabby's urinary tract problems as opposed to buying himself a new CD player or paint job for his truck. Why, with the leftover change alone, you could still go out and buy a brand new Tabby, if you so desire.

I'm not alone in thinking this way—a lot of men do. The only problem is, we don't dare admit it because women raise holy hell when the welfare of a pet is questioned. That's because the pet is "cute," or "adorable," or "cuddly" even though it may have just hawked up hairballs the size of jawbreakers. Women just adore pets, and won't even consider doing a Monica with you if you don't feel exactly the same way. So, we men disavow our dignity and common sense and go along with them.

It's time to consider the male's needs, though. The male ends up having to do the fun jobs associated with the ownership of the pet—throwing out the squirrel carcasses the cat killed (I just did that yesterday), scraping dried poop off hot asphalt, or smiling when the cat jumps into your lap and sinks its claws a good half-inch into your inner thighs. It's for these reasons, and many others, that the male looks at the pet situation much differently than the female does.

This said, I'm now ready to discuss the new entrepreneurial concept that I mentioned to you earlier. This is something that most male pet owners would welcome and cherish. I wish I could take credit for this profound concept, but I have to give credit where credit is due.

Remember the name Scotty Belk. Scotty is the originator of the profound concept that I'm about to explain here.

It all came up when I was over at Scotty's house several months ago. He was outside in his yard getting ready to cut the grass when I strolled up. We started shooting the breeze, and then I noticed that Scotty looked pretty worn out. When I asked if he was, he told me that he was totally ragged out due to lack of sleep. I, of course, then asked the totally innocent question as to why he didn't get any sleep during the night? (To be honest, I was hoping Scotty would give me some salacious details about all-night sexual escapades, but, alas, this proved not to be the case).

Scotty gave me a resigned look, and told me that he had gotten no sleep the night before. The reason for this was that his next-door neighbor's dog spent most of the night yapping right outside Scotty's bedroom window. He then added that the barking started around one A.M., and didn't conclude for the remainder of the night. In fact, the noise didn't stop until Scotty went outside at seven A.M. and launched a really large rock right by Barfy's head (no, he didn't hit the dog, nor was he really trying to—I don't want Scotty being picketed by animal rights activists just because he has a strong throwing arm).

Scotty then gave me a pensive, Foskey-type look and said, "What can you do about something like this? If you throw something at the dog or hose it down, everyone gets on to you like you're some kind of heathen. It's like the animal has more rights than you do. Think about it, Ed. If I went into someone's yard and took a dump in the grass, they'd have the law on me so fast that our heads would spin. But, let a dog do the same thing, and you're supposed to accept it and look the other way. It's a bunch of crap, I tell you."

I really couldn't disagree with Scotty. He seemed to be shooting pretty close to the target. I began nodding further agreement with him when he said, "The best answer to all this would be if you could just pay someone, in the middle of the night, to come over and shoot the damn dog. Just put it out of its misery. Then, the pooch goes to doggie heaven and I get some sleep."

I had to admit, and did out loud, that this was a profoundly new concept. As we further discussed it, the genesis of a potential new business idea sprung forth. We decided that we would call this business Pet Assassins.

What a concept! Think about it. When you've gotten to the end of your rope, when the barkin' or crappin' or meowin' has gotten to be too much, you put a swift and definitive end to the problem. A call to Pet Assassins, Inc., solves your dilemma. The situation is taken care of, no problems between neighbors engendered, and the serene life you were living continues onwards. It was a great idea, so much so that as Scotty and I kept talking about it, we joked about working up a list of potential services and prices.

"I guess there'd have to be a price differential based on what you used to kill the pet with. I'd charge more if I had to use an expensive gun," Scotty said.

"Yeah, and you'd have to charge more if they wanted the carcass hauled away," I added. "You'd have to offer that service. What if the owners wake up and see that their pet has been shot? They'll go nuts and call the cops immediately. It won't take long for the police to figure out that a neighbor ordered the hit and, when that happens, you're as good as caught. Think about how they'll treat you at work when you're exposed as a pet assassin. Worse yet, think about being in church and the preacher giving a pointed sermon on animal abuse. Nothing could be worse than that."

Scotty said then that maybe a pet assassin business wasn't necessary, that maybe you could just kidnap pets and then distribute them through an underground pet adoption service. It was a noble thought, but I told him that it just wouldn't work. I figured that it would be impossible to get into someone's backyard in the middle of the night and wrestle a big

German shepherd into a bag or something. I continued to muse on this when Scotty said, "Damn, Ed, you wouldn't do that. You'd just use one of those dart guns like they used to use on *Mutual of Omaha's Wild Kingdom*. You'd just nail the pet with a dart full of sleeping potion, bag it, and BOOM, yer outta there!"

Okay, I could see that. Made a lot of sense, too. We were getting even more elaborate in our scheming when Scotty's wife happened to walk outside. In order to avoid getting verbally reprimanded due to the subject matter of our discussion, we stopped talking about it and switched over to discussing turf fungus problems or something.

Just remember, you heard it here first. Pet Assassins, Inc.—the most innovative business concept to come along in years. Sure, it might be a tad much for the squeamish, but for the hell-bound entrepreneur it could prove to be one of the most lucrative business ventures ever. Think it's too bizarre? Just wait 'til next time when old Barfy on the next lot starts payin' off outside your window at 3 A.M. See then if you don't wish you could just pick up your phone book and let your fingers do the walkin'.

Georgia Tech 21, Georgia 19

Believe me when I tell you that I'll never write any words sweeter than the ones you just read—Georgia Tech 21, Georgia 19.

We just got through (11/28/98) playing a little football game here. One that we engage in each year around this time. The Game. Or let's just call it like it is—the Game of ALL Games.

No game in football matters more, you know. Not the Super Bowl, not the Orange Bowl, Rose Bowl, or whatever else is out there. This is the game that counts—the Tech/Georgia game.

You'd have to live here to understand. Now, don't get me wrong, I know there are lots of good college football rivalries out there. Games like Auburn/Alabama, Clemson/South Carolina, Florida/Florida State, etc. All these games are huge in their respective regions. (I won't even mention rivalries involving northern schools here. To be frank, it's hard for us Southerners to get upset about the big northern college rivalries. Let's face it, we don't give a tinker's damn about who wins between Ohio State and Michigan, Harvard and Yale, or whomever. The way I see it, just let 'em play the game and enjoy the fact that one of them is gonna get an ass-whuppin'. And understand that the only thing better would be if both teams could receive one. But we all know they can't, so I content myself with the fact that one will get one. Southerners in general are always glad about that, and will typically pull for the highest-ranked team in the game to tote the collar on any given Saturday. This helps insure that a good Southern team will rise a few more notches in the national rankings).

But none of these games is as huge as Georgia Tech and Georgia. These two schools started hooking up on the gridiron in 1893. Since then, they have waged an annual war each year around Thanksgiving. Families divide their loyalties on this day. It's not uncommon on game day to see a family attending the game with members wearing the colors of both schools. It's a day that divides this state in half for four hours, and introduces fans of both universities to either profound happiness or depression for the next 364 days.

There are a lot of myths associated with this game. Lots of lies are told, too, that people want to disguise as myths. If you really think about it, I guess most of us Georgians don't want the level of true hatred surrounding this rivalry to be exposed. It isn't very becoming to admit hate, I guess. But, if you think about it, pure hatred has its place and is very necessary at times. And where Tech and Georgia are concerned, it's damn necessary. Therefore, with all this reasoning behind me, I feel it's now time to give you the facts regarding the Tech/Georgia rivalry. I will accomplish this by exposing three of the most common myths surrounding the Tech/Georgia game.

Myth One: "I pull for both teams each year until they play each other. Then, I pull for (fill in the blank)."

This is a damn lie. Let's just get it straight, and duly noted on paper—no true Tech fan pulls for Georgia. In any shape, size, or form. If Georgia played the Iraqi Army I'd be wearing a Saddam Hussein t-shirt. Good Georgia fans will tell you the same thing—they hate Tech. And that's as it should be. That means things are in harmony, just as nature intended. Anyone who says differently is probably one of those tree huggers who thinks a frog is more important than a person. 'Sides, a good case of hate is good for one's metabolism—that's why watching the Tech/Georgia game is part of a good preventive health program. Keeps the system cleansed of impurities.

Myth Two: "This is not our biggest rivalry each year. Now, because of our conference schedule, when we play (fill in the blank), that's the big game!"

Georgia fans always tell this lie whenever they've fluked out and actually beaten Tech a time or two. Whenever that happens they all want to make out like there's no rivalry between the two schools at all. They'll start talking instead about games like the Georgia/Florida game (which is surprising, as Florida has been filleting their asses for the past several years like free steaks in a soup kitchen), or the Georgia/South

Carolina one (which S.C. would win if Captain Kangaroo was their quarterback), or others. It's just their means of building up some kind of inner feeling of superiority over Tech. I guess they need this, as after graduation most Georgia alumni will then spend a lifetime working for Tech grads. However you cut it, this delusion works out just fine for them until they lose the big game.

When they lose it, you know it, and quickly. The most obvious signs:

1. Whining about the officiating. This year it was the whine that their quarterback, in the second quarter, made a two-point conversion that was not counted by the officials. If they had made it, this year's match-up would have ended in a tie. Bottom line, we Tech fans know that we are doing well when Georgia supporters are bawling for the tie.

2. Coach Donnan's (who's since lost his job over losing thrice to Tech) television show replaying the Tech/Georgia contest becomes so loaded with commercials that game clips and commentary regarding the outcome are minimal.

3. Lots of talk about how they had to let us win one, and constant references to the number of games they had won in a row before this year. I always wonder what their point is here—no one gives a damn about what Chester A. Arthur did as president, and no one cares about old Georgia win hash-ups, either.

4. Increased Budweiser sales in the Athens area from the date of the game until after the ending of whatever bowl game Tech is in that year.

5. Complaints from Vince Dooley about damage to the hedges.

6. Increased donations from Tech fans to UGA in the name of Professor Jan Kemp.

I could even live with some of these lies if they were more creative, but, considering their sources, they can't be. Let's just conclude it to say that if you think Georgia fans really believe that any other game is their main rivalry, wait and talk to 'em about ten minutes after Tech has raked their cardsacks. You'll find out at that point, as the six excuses listed above are solemnly rattled off, that it still is, and will always be, The Game.

Myth Three: "Tougher academic standards at Georgia make it more difficult to field competitive teams."

Georgia fans are still solemnly stating this adage, which began back in the seventies when Professor Jan Kemp sued the university. I can't remember the exact details of the lawsuit, but essentially she sued the school, stating that she and other professors had to give preferential academic treatment to "student athletes" who, altogether, had the collective

IQ of a truck full of BB guns. She won her suit, collected over a million bucks, and thereafter incurred the everlasting wrath of true Georgia football devotees.

Georgia fans have clutched at this lawsuit as a way of explaining every loss they've suffered since. They'll intone this adage almost reverently, but, if you examine it, it begs the following questions: What's wrong with tougher academic standards? Does the school want to turn out a bunch of degree-toting, second-shift Dairy Queen management trainees? How can academic standards even be mentioned after a Tech/Georgia game? Even the most diehard Georgia fan doesn't want to go there.

Let's face it, any school that would rely on this kind of logic is not one we'd want to train future brain surgeons or airline pilots. I could say more, but let's sum it up by saying that Georgia fans who recite and believe this statement are being just as humorous as when we hear a recent Democratic president tell us that he is being truthful.

There are a lot more myths about this rivalry, to be sure, but some of them are so ridiculous that I can't even make fun of them. They do that on the strength of their own absurdity. Just bet the bank on one thing—the Tech/Georgia rivalry is the strongest in all of college football. The schools hate each other. And I love hating Georgia, just like Georgia fans love hating Tech. And beyond that, all you folks what don't live in Georgia leave us the hell alone. We have a right to this hatred, and we will steady kick some out-of-state ass if we are denied this sacred sacrament of Georgia living.

Chapter 10
MEETIN' BTO

☾

You're telling me that Ray and Hugh
are sharing sleeping accommodations?
— Robbin Bachman

This was bound to happen . . . .
The best damn rock band in the world meeting the world's
most elite social organization. BTO, the band that gave us "Roll On
Down The Highway," "Not Fragile," "Takin' Care Of Business," and
"You Ain't Seen Nothing Yet." The Brotherhood, (Ray, Hugh, and I),
livers of life and tellers of tall and slightly off-color tales. There we
were, all together, and on stage in Charleston, South Carolina.

It damn sure happened. And was, without question, the best road trip
in the Brotherhood's illustrious history. We still talk about it now—it's
the standard all future road trips will be measured by. And, as I write
this, we are only about two months away from going to see BTO rock
the house again, this time in Beaufort, South Carolina.

You have to understand something as I write this. Kids in Juliette,
Forsyth, or Adrian, Georgia don't get to meet their rock idols. They just
don't. When you grow up in the sticks as far out as all of us did, meeting your rock idols was like waiting for piss to turn to butter—it's just
never gonna happen. For us to get this opportunity was the real chance
of a lifetime, and one for which we will be forever grateful.

I can vividly remember the first time I heard, "Takin' Care of
Business." It was back in 1973, and I thought it was one of the best
songs I had ever heard. Then along came, "You Ain't Seen Nothing Yet."
That was even better. I loved the buzz-tone power chords in the music,
the drumming, and the quirky voice of Randy Bachman.

Around 1976, I bought the eight-track tape version of *BTO's Greatest Hits—So Far*. It was then that I heard hits like "Roll On Down the Highway," "Let It Ride," "Blue Collar," and "Gimme Your Money, Please." I then discovered Fred Turner, a man who has one of the greatest voices in rock music. A voice that sounds like a sweet sledgehammer, pounding out the words that mix so well with the powerful music that accompanies them.

I was hooked. Hopelessly and gratefully hooked. Finally, a band that sounded like a man's band. A band that shook off pretense, let themselves rock, and rock hard. Damn hard. A band that didn't dress up like Tinker Bell or coat themselves in mascara. A band that had a masculine name—BTO, Bachman-Turner Overdrive. Bottom line, a band that a seventeen-year-old boy could be proud to say he liked. In front of anyone.

It wasn't always easy to like them. Let's face it, if you wanted to hone the proverbial tulip, they weren't the best band in the world to listen to. You could always score if you wanted to listen to wimpy shit like Chicago, Yes, or the Carpenters. Girls I went out with got distracted from the potential swapping of bodily fluids if BTO came on the radio. Their rhythm was so infectious that it distracted the normal hormonal flows that must occur between a teenage boy and girl if tulip honing is to even have the remotest chance of happening.

I can remember one such tender moment with Rita Mingler, a girl I took one evening to the Riverside Drive-In. It was a hot July night, and Rita had the reputation of being morally challenged. So morally challenged that the word around school was that not being successful with her on a date meant that you either had to have leprosy or breath that would approximate the smell of rotting corpses. In essence, Rita was the kind of girl that if everyone on earth died but two million men and one woman, she's the one you wanted to have available for breeding purposes. She would have performed her tasks with vigor and thoroughness.

I took Rita on the night in question and parked in a very secluded part of the drive-in parking lot. One of those back corners where there are weeds, potholes, discarded tires, and the like. Those spots at the drive-in that everyone knew were earmarked as prime tulip-honing acreage.

Once I parked my car, I got out and did something very debonair. I pulled out a bottle of Windex and a rag, got out, and cleaned off my windshield glass. It's a great move because maneuvers like that assured your date that you were kind, considerate, and basically there to see the movie. It was a crock of shit, but it worked if you wanted a chance at her drawers. So, I cleaned that damn windshield with gusto.

Once it was clean, I asked Rita if she wanted something to eat. She rattled off a helluva list of items—two hot dogs, fries, Cracker Jack, a snow cone, chips, etc. I started totaling up all the food costs in my mind, and I began to see that laying her was not gonna be a cheap proposition. I guess, though, that costs are costs, whether a man pays for his pleasure with diamonds, minks, cars, or Reese's Peanut Butter Cups.

I walked down to the concession stand and got in line. I must've waited for over an hour to pick up all that damn food she wanted. Finally, with two exhausted arms (and an exhausted wallet) full of food items, I walked back to my car over in the conjugal corner of the parking lot.

Rita didn't even wait for me to give her the food as she reached up and whipped a hot dog right off the top of the pile. Swallowed it whole in two gulps. At first, I was really worried that she was gonna ask me to go back for more food, then, I began to realize that the skill she had just displayed could have pleasurable consequences for me later on in the evening.

We sat there for about the first forty-five minutes just eating and watching the movie. I can't remember what the movie was, and there was a damn good reason for that. You see, the worst thing you could possibly do on a drive-in date was take your date to an interesting movie. If you did that, God forbid, she would want to watch the damn thing. The whole damn thing. And if she wanted to watch the whole movie, it inevitably meant that any thoughts you might have had of getting your love pencil sharpened could be thrown in the back seat along with your Windex bottle and rag. It just wasn't gonna happen.

With us, though, nature had begun to take its course. After we'd eaten, and after about an hour and a half of the movie had passed, things began to get more interesting. We began by kissing, softly at first, and then more like two eels glued together at the throat. From this we progressed into a groping of each other's bodies that had to be reminiscent of what a strip search in San Quentin must have been like.

Things were going pretty damn good, if I do say so myself. That's when, as I was beginning an attack on Rita's brassiere hooks, she moaned softly that, "Music makes me sooooo hot."

That's all it took for me. As one hand kept working those hooks, the other eased up to my radio dial and switched it on. Bad move for me, as the first thing that came out of my speakers was, "We be takin' care of business, every day. Takin' care of business, every way. Takin' care of business, it's all mine. Takin' care of business, and workin' overtime."

Then came those killer guitar and bass licks. Rita came right out of the hormonally induced trance that I was trying so desperately hard to get her into. She then breathed out, "Isn't this song just too damn cool?"

I agreed that it was, and tried unsuccessfully to get the situation back to where it had been just a minute or so prior. I worked my ass off to accomplish this, but, it just wasn't meant to be. Rita started swaying and humming to the music, to the point where my hand lost its toe-hold on her bra hooks. In fact, my whole hand just sort of slipped off her back, and ended up right back on my side of the seat.

I was somewhat pissed. All that money for food, all the hard work, and for what? So these Canadian musicians could charm Rita back into her pants? I was really mad, and have to admit that at that particular point I was not real enamored with BTO.

Not that any of that mattered to Rita. She swayed and sang along with the entire song, and, when it ended, demanded that we leave immediately and go to a record store to pick up a copy of it.

I was redder than a snake's gut at that point, and told Rita that she had more chance of seeing me paint my ass pink than she did of me buying her a record. Buy her a record? Hell, I'd spent almost fifteen dollars feeding her bottomless-pit stomach, engaged in conversations that made a discussion of Plato seem exciting, and for what? So that we could go buy her a forty-five of "Takin' Care of Business?" I don't think so.

At times like this, chivalry demands that you not tell your date the truth about why you're taking her home. You can't tell her that you're basically mad 'cause you didn't get to examine the inner stitching of her panties, so I told her that one of those hot dogs I'd eaten had given me a good case of the skitters and we had to get home. Rita seemed to buy that, and rewarded my "honesty" by continually humming "Takin' Care of Business" the entire way back.

I finally got her home, said goodnight to her (she wouldn't kiss me goodnight as she was afraid I had a stomach virus—taught me not to use that alibi out on a date again), and made my way back to Juliette, forlorn and in possession of a huge male hormonal backlog.

A funny thing happened on the way back, though. As out of sorts as I was with the events of the evening, damned if I didn't catch myself humming "Takin' Care of Business" a couple of times. I couldn't help it. It had sort of an infectious quality to it that made the music keep running through my brain. Hell, it was simple enough that I figured even I could sing it—and so I did, in my car. Did a fairly decent job too, if I do say so myself.

You know you love a band when, over the years, you've bought their music in four different formats. God, it hurts to say that (from an aging standpoint), but it's true. I've purchased BTO albums on vinyl, eight-track tapes, cassettes, and now compact discs. You realize how damn old you're getting when you acknowledge salient facts like that.

Now, let's bring this story into the present, or, at least, closer to the present. It's April of 1998 and I'm about two months away from the release of *Sex, Dead Dogs, and Me: The Juliette Journals.*

At that point, I was incredibly scared. The book was the only thing I'd ever written in my life, and it was close to coming out for all the world to see. To be frank, I wrote it thinking that not more than a hand-ful of people would ever see it. It was just something I did to fool around and have fun. Instead, I was now in a situation where I felt like I had lost control—it was like I was about to drop my pants in front of the entire world, let everyone see my dimpled bottom, and had no hope of getting my britches back up in time to prevent it.

One thing I did often during that time was surf the internet. I'm a big internet fan. I love the Web, the capabilities of e-mail, and even allowed myself to become a chat-room junkie at one point (thank God I got beyond that—chat-room people, for the most part, comprise some of the strangest people you'll ever meet). That was a strange time. I did meet, in chat rooms, authors on the Web who were invaluably helpful to me. Nice people like Rebecca Paisley, Kelly Milner-Halls, and Linda Bleser first come to mind. I also met some weird writer types there. One lady wrote about the maladies of her cats and blamed their problems on the government. There was also an unusual person who occasionally came in the channel from Kansas. She'd published one five-buck sus-pense novel and would occasionally pop into our chat channel and loudly announce her presence there. Once announced, the people in the channel would proceed to fawn all over her. I always wondered why that happened. I respect suspense writers, but these cheapo jobs are not going to make the *New York Times* bestsellers list or be remembered as great works of literature. The only thing I could figure was that she was published, and that was all that really mattered to some of these people. They were like literary on-line groupies and just wanted to chat with a published author. That's one weird thing I've learned about writing—some people just love to kiss a published author's ass, even if the only thing he's ever published is a laxatives reference manual. Go figure.

Anyway, I was sitting around one night and decided that I would surf the Web. I hit the icon on my Web browser and away it went. I looked at all my favorite pages—www.ed-williams.com (blatant plug), Scoops Pro Wrestling Headlines, Danni's Hard Drive, and some others. After awhile, I decided I wanted to do some real Web surfing.

I went to one of my favorite search engines and starting thinking about what I wanted to research. Then it hit me—BTO, the best damn band in the world! I was sure there had to be a lot of stuff out there about them, and I wanted to get updated on what they were doing. I didn't know if the band still toured, who was in the current line-up, or anything else that was going on with them. The more I thought about all this, the more I wanted to read.

I loaded "BTO" into the search engine and hit the button. After a couple of seconds, all sorts of hits started ringing up. Apparently BTO was still well remembered by lots of fans if you judged by the number of sites that either were devoted to or mentioned them. There were tons of them.

I read through a couple of the BTO Web pages. After perusing them, I was pleasantly surprised to see that BTO was still a fully functioning band and in demand all over the world. The pages noted that the current BTO line-up consisted of Robin Bachman—drums; Fred Turner—vocals and bass; Blair Thornton—guitars; and Randy Murray—vocals and guitars.

From what I remembered, this was the line-up from their glory years, save Randy Murray, who joined the band in 1991. I kept reading this one particular BTO page until I saw something that riveted me: Robin Bachman's e-mail address!

No, I thought, this just couldn't be. I was convinced that someone was pulling a prank. There was no way in hell that this could really be Robin Bachman's e-mail address.

I went on about what I was doing, but the thought kept recurring, What if it really is his e-mail address?

I decided that it was crazy to keep thinking about it so much. The best thing to do was whip out a brief e-mail, send it, and see if it really was him. So I did. I wrote him a quick note and told him how much I had enjoyed the band over the years and mentioned that I had a book about to come out with several BTO references in it.

When I finished the e-mail, I hit the send button and immediately became embarrassed. I figured it had to be a hoax e-mail addy, and that I would soon start getting e-mails from every con job going on the internet. I could imagine the receiver of my e-mail laughing and saying, "Look at this dumb Southern ass. Sending an e-mail to Robin Bachman. We'll send him a note and tell him how he can buy a luxurious time share condo in Opp, Alabama—only fifty-eight miles from a concert venue BTO performed at in 1977."

Yeah, that would be my luck. I was pretty much convinced that I'd played hell when I went to bed. Robin Bachman's e-mail address? E-mail address my ass. It had to be a fake.

The next morning came, and after shaving and showering, I decided to log onto the internet and check my e-mail before going to work. I went through a few fairly routine ones when I saw, "BTORocks@aol.com."

My eyes bulged out—BTORocks@aol.com? It just couldn't be, but there was only one way to find out. I clicked on the e-mail folder and got the following message:

From: BTO ROCKS <BTOROCKS@aol.com>

To: Ed Williams <elwiii@mindspring.com>

Subject: Re: new book with BTO references

Yes, I sure would like a copy of the book. I hope that someone in Hollywood will make a movie of it. Then there will be a big BTO resurgence. That would be wonderful. We could re-record BTO hits for the sound track, wow, just think. If you are contacted about a movie I will be happy to help with the BTO stuff. Thank you so much for the honor of influencing your life and including us in your book. If you hear of BTO performing in or close to where you are, "E" me or our agent at blahblah@blah.com and get in touch with me for backstage passes. Robin

I just about crapped the proverbial golden brick, and added some silver mortar to boot. Robin Bachman sending me an e-mail? No way in the world, man. It just wasn't possible, but, damned if there it was, sitting right up there on the screen in front of my now staring eyes.

I was excited, and immediately went to a phone and called Ray and Hugh. I told them all about what had happened with Robin Bachman. They were as happy as I was, and congratulated me profusely. I then took a copy of my e-mail to work, where several of my coworkers read it, smiled, and nodded approval when they saw who it was from. At that moment, my book had already achieved more for me than I ever could have imagined. I'd gotten a real, honest-to-God message from Robin Bachman! Life couldn't have gotten much better for me than if all the sweet gum burrs in my backyard had suddenly, magically turned themselves into gold.

When I got home that evening, I figured the nice thing to do would be to e-mail Robin and thank him for being such a nice guy. I also wanted him to know about all the comments and reactions I'd gotten from my friends at work. With those thoughts in mind, I wrote him a quick e-mail, sent it, and forgot about it.

Forgot about it until the next morning. For when I logged into my computer, there was yet another e-mail message from Robin Bachman.

I was amazed all over again and read his message. Basically, it concerned the fact that he was glad people remembered and still highly regarded BTO, and he reminded me that he wanted to be kept informed as to what was going on with the book. I sent him a quick note back, and got my butt on to work.

From this point forward we began corresponding an average of two to three times a week. I had to keep reminding myself that this was Robin Bachman, charter member of BTO (the best damn band in the world), and that I was actually talking to him on an almost daily basis. It was nearly as good as getting a free front-row seat at a mud-wrestling exhibition.

I learned all sorts of things about Robin through these e-mails. He has an artistic side (designed the world famous BTO gear wheel logo), loves the worldwide touring the band still does, and likes to hit the strip clubs. This last item alone impressed the hell out of both Ray and Hugh. I also found Robin noteworthy because of his honesty. He answered any questions I asked of him forthrightly and offered insights if I seemed confused with his answers. I found him to be a normal, down-to-earth guy, who was honest as hell.

It was inevitable after all this e-mailing that we would begin discussing getting together during one of the band's tour stops. After checking out their summer 1998 tour dates, we found that the closest BTO would get to Georgia would be a date they had in Charleston, South Carolina, on Friday, June 12th.

When I received this information, I quickly relayed it to Ray and Hugh. After about fifteen seconds worth of intense discussion, we unanimously decided that a Brotherhood road trip was in order. Our trip-planning process then began. Hugh, being the Brotherhood's master of logistics, began making the decisions so necessary for a successful Brotherhood road trip experience.

What Hugh does before we go out on the road is check the convenience stores to determine who has the lowest prices for beer, the smallest Lotto lines, and most importantly, a place that doesn't have anyone on the payroll who knows one of us. When he determines this, we know we have found the establishment that the pretrip supplies will be purchased.

The pretrip supplies are a Brotherhood ritual and are very critical for a successful road trip experience. All eventualities must be taken into consideration and planned for, so that the members travel in matchless style and comfort.

Because we get asked about this all the time, here is the manifest for a Brotherhood road trip, and the members who typically utilize said supplies:

Beer: Ray, Hugh

Zimas: Me

Chips to go with the beer: Ray, Hugh, Ed

Cough drops to mask beer breath: Ray, Hugh, Ed

Two bags of sunflower seeds: Ray, Ed

Ice: Ray, Hugh, Ed

Air freshener: Whomever drinks the most beer

Hank Williams, Jr., cassette tape: Whoever is saddest

Ginseng extract: Whomever desires divorce

Packet of toilet paper: Whomever consumes large quantities of beer, chips, and cough drops before a long stretch of no gas stations

With these supplies in hand, and a full tank of gas and a road map, we are all ready to roll on down the highway.

On the morning of June 12th, the Pip and Hugh met over at my house. We all got into Hugh's Ford pickup, fired up the engine, and left my driveway headed for Charleston. I guess we'd gotten about a mile or so from my house when a warning light began shining on Hugh's dashboard, and a beeping sound began as well.

"Damn American-made piece of shit!" our patriotic brother Hugh exclaimed. After more obscenities, he informed us that this problem had been going on for several days, and that he wasn't entirely sure as to what was actually wrong with his truck. He then added, in pensive tones, that he was also not real sure if we could make it to Charleston in it or not.

I turned to Hugh and informed him that we could not miss out on BTO due to his clunker. Brother Pippin seconded that sentiment, and we all turned around and headed back to my house. Brother Foskey may have had his feelings damaged, but this was BTO and we were not going to be denied.

Back at my house, we loaded up our stuff into the Pip's Mercedes and exited my driveway again. We went a few miles down the road, stopped at Hugh's convenience store of choice, secured the manifest, and then rolled again on down the highway.

Our trip to Charleston was pretty uneventful, at least for the most part. There was one little incident on a parcel of deserted highway about ten miles from the South Carolina line. While riding over this stretch, Brother Foskey politely announced that he had to unleaven his bladder. We drove around forever trying to find a gas station, but there wasn't one to be found. As the beads of sweat began accumulating on Hugh's forehead, I started quoting statistics about the incredible amount of water that pulses down Niagara Falls each day. As he cursed me over quoting these particular stats, Brother Pippin stepped in and said, "Hugo, it doesn't look like you're gonna find a pot to piss in out here. Let's just pull over, open your door, leave it open, and just piss behind it. No one will see you doing it. We can just act like you're looking at an airplane or something."

Hugh was so desperate for relief that he went along with Ray's suggestion. He got out on the passenger side, faced the car door, and began pissing towards it. By doing this, his back was facing cars coming up on the opposite side of the highway. Ray noticed that Hugh was whizzing pretty closely to his car door and said, "This ain't no litter box, Foskey. Keep that python cocked downwards."

Hugh laughed so hard at this comment that he accidentally pissed a little on the bottom edge of Ray's car door. When he observed this, the Pip cussed some but generally seemed unperturbed. This mood ended when Ray noticed a large Greyhound bus quickly coming down the highway towards us on the opposite side of the road.

Ray turned, looked at me, and yelled, "Hold on!" With that, he threw the car in reverse, quickly moving us backwards thirty to forty yards. The net effect of this was that Brother Foskey was now standing out in the open with his dick in his hand, pissing like a swollen burro for all the world to see. Or, in this case, for all of the occupants of a Greyhound bus to see, as they were fastly approaching the awesome Foskey golden shower display.

"You sons of bitches!" Hugh yelled as he approached our car, his dick still firmly in his hand. Hugh got within ten feet of us when the Pip looked in his rear view mirror again, and, seeing no cars approaching, he proceeded to back her up yet another twenty or so more yards.

I busted out laughing at this sweet development. So did all the riders on the Greyhound bus that then proceeded to ride by the Fosk. Conversely, Hugh was cussing like a White House intern, but kept steadily running towards our car. Ray and I got to laughing harder as it hit us that Hugh was not aware that he was doing all this running with his dick in his hand. After awhile Hugh realized why Ray and I were laughing, and why he was also feeling an unusual amount of wind on his cucarachas. Tossing several more well-chosen cuss words to the Pip and me, he returned nature's Oscar Meyer frank to its rightful resting place within his designer logo britches.

Hugh got back in the car, complaining that he had a bad case of windburn of the dick. The Pip and I, showing our brother true compassion, gave him a medicinal cold beer and turned up the radio volume (we found us a good oldies station) so that we didn't have to hear his complaints. Then, we all began rollin' on down the highway again.

We eventually got into Charleston around one o'clock, all three of us half starving to death. After swinging up and down one or two of the main drags, we found a buffet-type place to eat lunch at. We all went in, ate, erased their profit margins, and got back into the Pip-mobile.

Our final destination for this trip was the Charleston Hilton. We picked this hotel because Robin told me the band was staying there, and we figured the whole thing would be logistically easier to handle if we were staying at the same hotel the band was.

All this was well and good, the only rub being the fact that we only had one hotel room reserved for the three of us. I mentioned that our sleeping arrangements might be difficult. Ray and Hugh laughed it off by pointing out that we would probably be out late partying, and would only have time for a few hours' sleep anyway. What difference would it make if we slept on a chair or something? I thought it made a helluva lot of difference, but in the Brotherhood the majority rules. I looked at Ray and Hugh, who both had pensive looks going, which led me to believe that further discussion regarding this matter was futile.

The three of us walked into the front lobby and the Pip promptly checked us in. While standing around, I noticed an area where newspapers were available. I walked over to where they were, got one, and started checking in the entertainment section to see if any articles were in there regarding the big concert. After a few minutes of perusal, I saw an ad that stated, "Charleston Birthday Celebration Concert—Featuring BTO and Jerry Lee Lewis"

BTO and the Killer? Together? I couldn't damn believe it! The mother of all concerts! If I were going to design a concert, this would be it. I gave a silent prayer of thanks to God for allowing me to enjoy this music, and, I also thanked him for allowing me to be a member of the Brotherhood.

I walked over and showed the ad to Hugh and Ray. They were also very excited about the prospect of seeing BTO and the Killer together. We then got our stuff collected and walked over to the elevators.

Our room was up on the tenth floor. When we got off the elevator and walked in, we discovered that there were two double beds inside. When we saw that, we then tried to decide how we were gonna set up the evening's sleeping arrangements.

"Foskey, you're the youngest member, you gotta sleep in those two chairs. E and I are gonna take the beds!" suggested Brother Pippin.

"Like bloody hell you are," responded Hugh pensively. "My dick is still chapped by that Olympic marathon y'all made me run. If I sleep in those chairs, the air conditioning vents will blow right on me, and my dick will be sorer than a short-changed whore in the morning."

"Well, one thing's for certain," I offered. "Since I'm the man that knows the band, and the senior member of the Brotherhood, one of these beds is reserved for me."

I figured Ray and Hugh would raise hell about that, but, oddly enough, they didn't question it (when I asked them later about it, they just both commented that they respected seniority). That narrowed the issue down as to who would get the other bed, Ray or Hugh.

Hugh started acting in an exaggeratedly effeminate way, and suggested that he would gladly sleep with the Pip. Ray laughed, and then told Hugh that he was about to put on his swim trunks and go cop some zzz's out by the pool. Hugh seemed to like this particular idea as well, so, both of them put on their trunks and got ready to go down into the water.

I wanted to do the same thing, but since I was the guy who knew Robin, I had the task of contacting him and seeing what we were all gonna do that evening. Given that, I sat back, flipped on the TV, and watched my brothers leave the room to go lounge around the pool. As soon as the door shut behind them, I began calling Robin. After two hours or so, I finally got him on the phone.

"Robin?"

"Yes, this is Robin."

"Hey man, this is Ed."

"No shit, with that accent who else could it be?"

I laughed and told him we'd all made it into town. He told me that was great, that the band looked forward to meeting the infamous Brotherhood, and that we could all meet at five P.M. in the lobby and have some dinner in the hotel restaurant.

I was excited as all hell when I hung up—dinner with BTO! I immediately hopped on the elevator and made my way down to the ground floor. Once there, I looked all over the lobby area trying to discover where the damn pool was. After about ten minutes or so of looking, I found it and marched out to poolside to locate the Pip and Hugh.

Finding them was easy—they'd pulled two lounge chairs together and had a six pack of beer in a tiny ice chest between them. As I got closer, I noticed both of them had enough sunscreen on to lubricate the entire cast of a porno flick. As I strolled up, the Pip was innocently saying, "You know Fosk, a few more of these brewskis and I might have to walk over there and tell that blond lady in the purple bikini that she has too much ass for that thong. You can't even see it 'cause of those two big, mushy cellulite cheeks being mashed together."

That thought alone was enough for me to lose my appetite, but, nonetheless, I proceeded to inform Hugh and Ray about our BTO dinner invitation. Hugh thought I was lying at first, but Ray told him that I wouldn't lie about something regarding BTO. Hugh accepted that logic, so the two of them got up, eyed the purple bikini lady one last time, and went upstairs to get ready for dinner.

Once we got to the room, Ray started peeling off his clothes to get ready to shower. I sat back and watched TV as I really didn't need one, and Hugh kept talking about how surreal this whole situation was. The Brotherhood, three middle Georgia country boys, getting ready to eat dinner with BTO. It just boggled the mind. This conversation was picking up steam when The Pip, now as naked as ten jaybirds, said, "Hugh, are you going to get in the shower with me?"

"Hell no, I'm not getting in the shower with you!" Hugh replied.

"You may as well, Hugh. The way I see it, you can either get in there with me and make it easy on yourself now, or, when we get into bed later my best advice for you would be to sleep on your back!"

Hugh and I just howled with laughter. Hugh and the Pip together in the shower? Both of them had been doing this effeminate shtick since we'd arrived earlier in the afternoon. I think they got the idea for it when it occurred to both of them that they just might be sleeping together in the same bed later on in the evening. I busted out laughing from imagining the prospect of seeing those two in bed together.

Ray finished his shower, Hugh caught one too, and all three of us were ready for dinner just a few minutes before five. We got in the elevator and rode down, strolled out in the lobby, and waited around for BTO to show up.

It didn't take long for that to happen. After just a few minutes, I saw this guy walking through one of the hotel's side lobby entrances. He was wearing gym shorts, sneakers, and a t-shirt with a BTO logo on it. It was Robin Bachman in the flesh. I'd seen too many album covers not to know who he was. I immediately walked over and stuck my hand out, "Robin, I'm Ed Williams."

"Nice to meet you, Ed. It's obvious you already know who I am," Robin laughed.

"Man, it's good to see you. I tried calling you earlier in the day, but I couldn't get ahold of you 'til four."

"Well, we had to do sound checks, then some interviews, and all that kept us pretty well tied up most of the afternoon. I can already see one thing is gonna go better than I thought."

"What's that?"

"The fact that I can understand your ass without an interpreter. Damn Ed, I've heard some strong Southern accents but yours sounds like a Southern accent with syrup poured on top of it."

I had to laugh like hell at that, and reminded Robin that in South Carolina my accent was gonna be much more easier for people to handle than his was. He admitted that I had a point, and then said the magic words, "I'm hungry—ready to eat, man?"

I definitely wanted to eat, but first, "Robin, I need to introduce the Brotherhood to you. This is Hugh Foskey, better known as 'The Fosk,' and Ray Pippin, known far and wide in these parts as 'The Pip.'"

"Hello, Fosk and Pip. I'm hungry, aren't you?"

Everyone nodded, so we all walked in and took our seats at one of the tables. Small talk was exchanged over the next several minutes when I then noticed another person walking through the restaurant entrance.

Fred Turner! It was Fred Turner himself! God, I am such a fan of the man's. He has an unbelievable voice—one of the strongest and most powerful in the history of rock 'n' roll music. The man who made songs like "Not Fragile" and "Roll On Down The Highway" the classics they are. I'll tell you here and now, it's worth the price of admission just to go to a BTO concert and hear Fred sing "House of the Rising Sun." You may think you've heard this song before, but you'll never hear it sung like you will when Fred gets in front of it.

Fred walked right on over and sat down. He immediately introduced himself to all three of us, and joined right into our conversation. After talking with him for a few minutes, one thing struck me. Here was this man, a physically large man with one of the strongest voices in rock music history, barely talking above a whisper. It was such a contrast. If you visualized Fred as you hear him on a record, you'd think he was a loud, bangin' kind of guy. The reality of it is that he's an extremely gentle, congenial, soft-spoken man. He's one of those kind of people who will go to great lengths to please people and is incredibly down-to-earth. The respect I already reserved for him was skyrocketing upwards after only a few minutes of getting to know him.

We all talked and had the best time at dinner. I asked Robin and Fred a ton of BTO-related questions and mentioned to them that one of my favorite songs was a cut off their first album entitled, "Hold Back The Water." They looked at each other and mentioned something about working it into the show later that evening. Hugh kept Fred engaged in conversation, and Robin, Ray, and I talked a lot as well. In fact, this conversation was rolling right along until the moment Ray posed the following question to the guys, "Have y'all ever been audited by the IRS?"

You'd have thought that someone had just started charging restaurant patrons for air. Robin and Fred both got real quiet, but Robin ultimately replied, "That's a helluva question to ask right before dinner. Why do you ask it?"

"Cause I'm the best damn tax man in the business, and I can save a band's ass just like I can anybody else's," answered the Pip.

Everyone laughed heartily at the Pip's comment and continued on with their eating. I was having the time of my life, yet the whole situation kept seeming surreal to me. The Brotherhood eating dinner with members of BTO. Who would have thought? I kept looking at Robin and Fred, and my mind would go back to memories of their pictures on album covers. I also found the experience a little emotionally charged. I remember thinking how I wished I could tell those guys how much enjoyment they'd brought me over the years with their music. I didn't do that, though, as we had such a good, down-to-earth conversation going that I didn't want to lapse into fan-speak.

Before we realized it, dinner was over. I'd been talking so intently to those guys that I'd barely noticed how much time had passed. We all began getting up when it hit me that we didn't know what to do about the concert that evening. I mentioned this to Robin, and assured him that the three of us were more than willing to buy tickets. We just wanted to see the show and witness two of the greatest acts in rock music history.

Robin said that he was going to catch an hour or so of sleep, and that Fred was going over to the Coliseum to do another interview. Fred told me that he would go over, check things out, and call me in about twenty or so minutes. I told him that I really appreciated it, then we all shook hands and walked out of the restaurant together.

I told Ray and Hugh that I would go upstairs and wait for Fred to call. Ray and Hugh said that they would sacrifice as well and wait for me in the motel bar. Praising the two of them for this unparalleled act of sacrifice, I proceeded to get on the elevator, ride up to our room, and await my call from Fred.

I know this seems crazy, but I swear that exactly twenty minutes from when Fred said he would call, the phone began ringing. I quickly answered it, "Hello?"

"Ed, this is Fred. We're all going to leave from the hotel lobby at eight to go do the show. Why don't the three of you just ride over with us? We have room in our van."

I tried to act nonchalant as hell, and told Fred that it sounded like a plan to me. As soon as I hung the receiver up, I ran like a scalded dog to the elevator.

As soon as I arrived on the ground floor, I made my way over to the bar. I went in there and noticed that Ray and Hugh were over in a corner sipping brews and playing video poker. Since I'd never played myself, I sat down at one of the machines and put money in. Have you ever noticed that at times when you're in a big hurry that you'll get lucky at a game like this? I sure did. I hit blackjacks on my first three hands and ran up a seventy-five-dollar positive cash flow.

In fact, I was ready for another hand to be dealt when Hugh said, "E, what's the deal on the show? When do we need to leave?"

I was damn sure glad he asked that as a quick glance at my watch told me that it was ten minutes 'til eight! Just enough time for me to tell my brothers that we'd better get our asses on out into the lobby. At first, they thought I was kidding about riding over to the concert with BTO, but when I told them that I'd bet the dust off a monkey's ass on it, they believed me, and we all proceeded out into the main lobby area.

At eight P.M. sharp Fred, Randy Murray, and Blair Thornton walked into the lobby. Introductions were made all around, and the group of us small-talked for a few minutes. After that, Fred was called over and told he had a phone call.

Turns out the call was from Robin. He had slept a little longer than expected and told Fred that he would meet us all a bit later at the Coliseum. With that taken care of, the guys motioned us outside and towards their van.

Ray, Hugh, and I walked up to it, a large-body Ford Econoline van that they had rented at the airport. It was full of all sorts of musical equipment; in fact, it was so packed that I couldn't even see how BTO could fit in there, much less BTO and the Brotherhood. I mentioned this to Ray and Hugh, and, being chivalrous, we told the guys we would just follow them over in our car.

Randy Murray asked, "What kind of car are you guys in?"

Hugh responded that we were in Ray's Mercedes. Randy immediately noted that he would rather ride in the Mercedes than the van. Hugh told him normally it would be okay, but that when the Brotherhood was out on the road we typically ran into problems with women flinging themselves into our car when we stopped at red lights. He added that he didn't want Randy to get hurt if some overwrought woman jumped into our car and mashed him. Randy laughed like hell, we all proceeded to get in our vehicles, and took off for the show.

Fred drove the van for the guys, and we stayed right behind him. It was only a short drive from the Hilton to the concert arena (the North Charleston Coliseum), but it was packed with traffic lights. I laughed and mentioned to Hugh that we could have picked up about two hundred overwrought women with the number of stops we were having to make. Hugh responded that a Mercedes had a world-class suspension system and could handle the weight. In any event, we stayed right behind Fred and the guys and made our way over to the Coliseum.

The North Charleston Coliseum came up quickly on the right side— all three of us sucked in our breath when we first saw it. It's a huge building, and looks like it was only recently constructed. The most noticeable thing about it was the large, inverted flying saucer-shaped dome that covered the top of the building. It really did make you think that a large UFO had landed on the roof and was waiting to zap some earthlings.

"That's a big bastard right there," Ray noted, "almost as big as my ol' pink sea monkey. Remember Fosk, you can pay me now or pay me later."

We all rolled, but our laughter subsided when we pulled into the Coliseum parking lot. Fred and the guys were driving around to the back, and there seemed to be at least a couple of checkpoints armed with guards. I wondered out loud if we'd be allowed to pass through. Ray replied, "E. Fred will fix it, and if he doesn't, we'll just peel rubber and blast our way back there. I'm experiencing the rock-star life now, and I'll be damned if some security guard is gonna put an end to it! He'll have to deal with the great-great-grandson of Jeremiah Pippin if he does!" I laughed like hell at this. (The Pip and I for years have joked about Jeremiah Pippin. He is the made-up fictitious founder of Forsyth, Georgia, and has his place alongside other mythical Pippin legends like Black Cat Pippin, Snuff Box Pippin, and my all-time favorite, Meat Cleaver Pippin. Legend has it that Jeremiah Pippin tied on a load one night, got on his burro, and then rode around aimlessly. Towards morning he fell off his burro and then slept off the effects of the liquor. The spot where ol' Jeremiah touched down became Forsyth, Georgia, and the exact location where Jeremiah foundered is the spot where the courthouse is now located). Fortunately, Fred had talked to the two guards, and we were waved right on through their particular checkpoints.

We pulled into the back of the building, literally parking no more than about ten to twelve yards from its doors. We all piled out of our vehicles, and I went back to the trunk of Ray's car to get the copies of my book that I had autographed for the band and for Jerry Lee Lewis.

Once I had them, the three of us walked up to the door and were promptly granted admittance by the security people.

Inside, we veered right and noticed that we were in a large, concrete corridor with doors on either side. After walking a few yards, we came right up to a door that had a sign on it that read "BTO Dressing Room. Knock First. Then Wait."

We all knew that we were in the right place. The three of us hung around for a few minutes, then Fred poked his head out and told me that it was okay to bring the books on in.

I walked back into their dressing room and deposited the books on a small wall shelf. I also noticed that BTO had a nice spread of food displayed on a long table—all sorts of fruits, cold cuts, and other assorted morsels. If it hadn't been for the fact that this was BTO, I would've walked up and helped myself, but, since we're talking about the best damn band in the world, I muted my hunger pangs, wished the guys a great show, and walked out of their dressing room into the outer corridor.

As Ray, Hugh, and I stood around in the hallway talking, the building's security manager informed us that we had total backstage clearances, i.e., we could go anywhere in the building we wanted to. This sounded pretty good to us, so, we began walking around and exploring the unusual environment we now found ourselves in.

As we walked around and looked, I began hearing sounds—sounds that could only be coming from the Killer himself, Jerry Lee Lewis! He had just launched into his classic hit, "Drinkin' Wine Spo-dee-o-dee." Hugh mentioned that we should try to find the concert arena and watch the Killer performing his hits. Ray and I instantly agreed, so we all began opening doors and searching.

I opened a couple of hallway doors and started getting frustrated. This was akin to solving a Rubik's Cube just to be able to watch the Killer. I did keep looking around, and proceeded to pull open a couple more doors, when I blundered right into the concert arena! It was like, at that moment, eight thousand some odd pairs of eyes were staring straight at me. To be blunt, it shocked me enough that I almost expelled every major bodily fluid that it's possible to lose. This incredible scene was reminiscent of a sea of human beings, a sea that was swaying and singing along with one of the greatest rock 'n' roll icons of all time.

I looked to my left and saw the Killer at his grand piano—he couldn't have been more than fifteen yards away. Right next to him was James Burton, one of the most outstanding guitar players in the history of rock and roll music. Mr. Burton played lead guitar for Elvis when he resumed concert touring back in the early '70s, which tells you all you need to know right there. He was a legend in the music business, and here he was, punching out lead guitar solos a mere few yards away from me.

I stuck my head back out into the hallway, and yelled like hell for Ray and Hugh to join me. They came right over, walked out into the arena, and inhaled sharply when they saw the size of the assembled crowd. Once they had steadied themselves, they joined me by the side of the stage to watch the rest of this awesome concert.

It was all incredibly surreal. I was watching the man whose recording of "Great Balls Of Fire" I first listened to when I was two years old. Loved it so much that I learned how to play the forty-five on my mama's record player, and did so to the point that she grew to hate the song on account of the repetitions she had to endure. And now I was watching him accompanied by all the members of the Brotherhood. It was enough to put one on sensory overload.

The Killer proceeded to bang out "Great Balls Of Fire" and "Whole Lotta Shakin' Goin' On" to thunderous applause from the Coliseum crowd. Then, he slowly got up from his piano stool and made his way over to the exit steps from the stage. These steps happened to be right next to where the Brotherhood was standing, so we all instantly realized that we'd get to see Jerry Lee up close when he walked by.

As we waited for him to walk off the stage, I noticed a man with a shock of white hair walking up to the edge of those steps. It was Dr. Nick, George Nicholopolus, the man who rose to somewhat infamous fame as Elvis's doctor in the '70s. What made this even more surreal for me was that I noted Dr. Nick carrying the copy of *Sex, Dead Dogs, and Me* that I had autographed for Jerry Lee (I'd slipped the copy to the head of security backstage earlier).

Ray and Hugh noticed this too, and we were all oohing and ahhing over it. It was the wildest scene—Dr. Nick, Jerry Lee, James Burton. We all looked at each other and agreed that if a flock of buzzards swooped over our remains the next day that we would have no regrets, for we could say that we had been to the summit, and could achieve nothing more meaningful in our lifetimes.

The Killer made his way down the steps and walked right by us—his security detail wouldn't let you get real close to him. I smiled like hell when I saw Dr. Nick show the Killer the title of the book. He smiled, and I hoped that he might someday sit down and read a few chapters from it.

No time to dwell much on Jerry Lee, though. In about five minutes a local deejay walked up to the microphone, introduced himself, and quickly announced BTO to the gathered concert attendees.

The Coliseum audience went crazy with applause as Randy, Fred, Robin, and Blair walked up on the stage. They all got their instruments, nodded at each other, and counted off the first song.

The song was "Let It Ride," one of the many classic BTO hits from the seventies. And walking up to the microphone to deliver its lead vocals was the quiet, retiring man that I'd just had dinner with, the one so soft spoken that you could barely hear him at times during our conversations.

Hugh leaned over to me and whispered that we shouldn't get our hopes up too much, that a lot of years had passed since the seventies, and that the band might be way past its prime. This sentiment lasted until Fred began singing, "You can't see the mornin', but I can see the night . . . ."

God, he blasted out those words! It was as about as subtle as a semi full of hogs ramming into another filled with sulfur. Hugh's mouth dropped open, and he said "Goddamn! Can they rock? Hell, they may be better than when we first listened to them back at Napier Dorm in '76."

There wasn't time to discuss much else. These guys were just rocking the damn house, song after song after song. The energy level they all maintained was incredible. I loved how they unselfishly shared the spotlight with each other, and the professional teamwork that was so evident between them. I can remember thinking that the music industry needed to have its head examined if some major label wasn't having these guys whip out a new CD each year or so. The crowd seemed to feel that way, too, as they were rocking and jamming out with every single tune they did.

"Four Wheel Drive," "Not Fragile" (I want so badly to get on stage with them one day and just sing the *not fragiles* that Fred intersperses into the song), "Hold Back the Water," "Takin' Care of Business," "You Ain't Seen Nothing Yet," and "House of the Rising Sun."

Before singing that song, Fred told the crowd how the band had played a gig in the early seventies where a lot of motorcycle gang members were in attendance. Apparently, one of the earlier performing bands was supposed to sing "House of the Rising Sun" but didn't. BTO was the featured act that evening, and, as they were about to finish their set, they were approached by one of the gang members.

"When are you going to play 'House of The Rising Sun?'" asked the biker.

Fred told him that BTO didn't do the song.

The biker replied, "Well, if you don't do it, y'all can't leave."

Fred went on to say that it was amazing how quickly you can learn a song if the proper inspiration is there. BTO went on and performed "House of the Rising Sun" that night, and got a thunderous round of applause from the gathered bikers. Since then, they've made it a staple in all their live concert performances.

Fred then began singing it for the Charleston audience, and the entire crowd was transfixed. I can remember he delivered the vocals so powerfully that his face was beet red the entire time he sang it. Even the other members of BTO seemed to be listening to him. When he finished, the place just exploded and I think I saw one or two people in the audience blink back tears.

The band members then took a quick break. Well, all of them except for Robin. He stayed on stage and put on a virtuoso drumming exhibition. He must've drummed by himself on for a good fifteen minutes. He did rolls, beat the cymbals with his hands, and threw his drumsticks out into the crowd and did all the drumming with his bare hands. He got tons of applause, and I can remember marveling at the fact that his arms didn't fall off due to their exertions.

The rest of the band returned after Robin's solo and played a few more tunes, took bows, and then left the stage. When the crowd demanded an encore, they came back and performed "Roll On Down the Highway." After doing this number, they bowed for their fans and finally left the stage for good.

Ray, Hugh, and I left our positions next to the stage and found our way back to the band's dressing room. We stood a short distance off to the side, and noticed that several people were out there waiting for them as well.

After fifteen or so minutes the guys came out, signed autographs, and posed for pictures with their fans. They were also kind enough to sign their dressing room door sign for me. Then, Blair Thornton walked up and said, "Ed, sorry I didn't do so earlier, but I really want to thank you for my copy of the book. I do look forward to reading it."

I didn't even know what to say. I tried to thank him for all the great entertainment he had given me over the years. I'm sorry to say that I couldn't find the words. Then, without pause, he reached into his pocket and gave me four of his BTO logo guitar picks, and his personal backstage security clearance badge. I swear that if there hadn't been a lot of people around I would have fought back tears. Actually, I fought them back anyway.

Robin was still signing autographs, when I walked over and whispered to him that Ray, Hugh, and I would like to get a picture with the band. When I mentioned it, Robin looked at Randy, Fred, and Blair, and said, "Let's walk out on stage, and pose for a picture with the Brotherhood."

A picture of BTO and the Brotherhood onstage! I couldn't even imagine, but there we all were, proceeding to walk out and take one. The best damn band in the world and the most elite social organization in the world, about to be immortalized together on film. We all got up on the stage and sat on one of the nearby risers. I was between Fred and Robin, and Blair was to the right of Fred. Randy, Hugh, and Ray were right behind us. The local deejay took a couple of pictures using Hugh's camera.

Hugh leaned over and whispered, "E. we've been blessed tonight."

We had been, you know. How else could you look at it? It was a night to be remembered for the rest of our lives. Not much time to reflect on that, though. Robin looked at me and said, "We'll meet you guys back at the hotel lounge."

When he said that, Ray, Hugh, and I smiled broadly and replied that that was fine with us. We told the guys that we were gonna go ahead and leave, and would see them in the lounge a bit later.

The three of us strolled down those concrete corridors one last time, and found the back door exit. Looking out at the building one last time to preserve our memories, we all got into the Pip's car and made our way back to the Hilton in little or no time at all.

Back at the Hilton we went inside, made a beeline to the bar, and ordered some cold brews to sip on while we waited. We sat around and marveled at the events we had just experienced.

Pretty soon Randy Murray came in, and he and I immediately launched into an intense conversation about baseball. It turns out Randy is a huge Atlanta Braves fan. He loves the team with a passion and collects Braves logo merchandise with a vengeance. He honestly can't seem to get enough of it, so if all you BTO fans want to score points with Randy, just give him a t-shirt or jersey with a Braves logo on it. He'll be grateful forever.

A few minutes after Randy came in, Robin and Fred both appeared. We all then gathered around a big table, got a round of beers, and began talking. The conversations were varied. Ray asked Robin about life on the road and the various sexual sins he may have committed. I talked to Fred about why BTO isn't recording for one of the major labels—they're ten times better than some of the crap spewing out of the radio today. Hugh was trying to listen to all these conversations going on simultaneously. Randy Murray and I started talking about professional sports. It was a genuine free-for-all discussion.

More beers were consumed, and the conversations intensified. I started asking Robin questions about certain aspects of the band's history. Even though these questions were pretty pointed (I wasn't feeling very much pain), he answered them all honestly and directly. I guess that's the main thing I came to respect about Robin—he's honest, and very to the point. I now find it fun to just throw things out at him, just to see what his reactions might be.

Fred excused himself to call it a night, and we all said goodbye and thanked him profusely for being so kind to us. He told us he had enjoyed his experiences with the Brotherhood and added that we were welcome to come with BTO to Myrtle Beach the next day, where they would be playing at the House of Blues. After asking us to consider going, he walked away to go back to his room for some well-earned rest.

Hugh, Ray, and I looked at each other. Myrtle Beach? Watching another BTO concert? Ray looked at us and said, "I'll pick up the tab if y'all will go. Let's go to Myrtle Beach with them."

I was riding the fence 'cause I wanted to go but knew Debbie would be mad as hell if I did. Hugh, on the other hand, was expressing pensiveness to a degree that I had never witnessed before. He stayed silent for a few moments, then said, "Shit, I want to go. Only thing is, if I do Rosemary will divorce my ass. I'm supposed to be at a church, sponsored married, couples function tomorrow night."

The Pip stepped up to the plate, "You mean you would miss a night out on the road with BTO for a church married-couples function?"

"Well I wouldn't, but Rosemary just won't understand."

"Fosk, you gotta grow some balls bigger than raisins if you want to sample some of the finer things in life."

Hugh admitted this was all true, but mentioned that he was sort of in the doghouse with Rosemary over some untold recent indiscretions. On account of this, he felt that he had better go home the following day.

Ray gave it one last shot, "Hugh, if she divorces you over a BTO concert, I'll pay for your attorney. Hell, I'll even personally represent you if you like. After all, we're gonna be a whole lot closer after tonight."

We all busted out laughing. Robin and Randy were wondering what the deal was, so I cued them in on the fact that Ray and Hugh might be sleeping together that evening. That got them to laughing, and all of us made jokes about Ray's and Hugh's "evening of passion" that would get me arrested if I shared them with you here.

I was dying to talk with Robin about groupies. I've always heard that bands have wild women chasing them from town to town, and that they go to extreme lengths to give rock stars their tulips to hone. All I can figure is these women think it's a big deal to have sex with someone famous. That's got to be what makes them act the way they do. I said something to that effect to Robin. He nodded and told me that he'd even seen cases where women's husbands would offer their wives to the guys in the band. I had a hard time believing this and said so, but Robin swore it was true. When he did, Brother Pippin made a comment about rock 'n' roll being the greatest business in the world and wondered if he could learn to pick a guitar at his age.

Robin went on to relate some BTO groupie escapades to us, and his words made me remember something I'd witnessed earlier in the evening. While BTO was doing their show, I saw this late-thirties blonde just going crazy. She shook and shimmied to the music, and kept licking her lips. You could tell that if Robin, Fred, Blair, or Randy had approached her that she would have dropped her britches faster than Ed Jr. eats ice cream. I kept watching her intermittently during the concert, and she seemed to get more aroused as the show progressed. Towards the end, she was out in one of the aisles dancing like a lizard who has been placed atop a hot plate.

I mentioned all this to Robin. Then, I told him I should have cornered the woman, told her I was the BTO groupie manager, and then informed her that she would have to come over to my hotel room after the show and participate in a special audition to determine if she would make the grade as a BTO groupie. Robin said, "You mean you didn't? Damn, you failed the test!"

It turns out that I was actually being auditioned for the role of BTO groupie manager, and this was a live test to see how I would handle myself under pressure! I'm greatly saddened to tell you that I failed miserably, and thus ended my chance to become an important cog in the BTO tour machinery.

Time passed, and it got very late. It turned out that Robin had inadvertently hit one of his lower front teeth with a drumstick during the concert. When he did this, it knocked the cap completely off of the tooth. His agent had scheduled an eight A.M. trip to the dentist for him the next morning, and he told us that he'd better get on to bed and try to get a few hours of needed rest.

I hated to see him go. We all bid him goodbye and shook hands. He told me that he would keep in touch and expressed appreciation for the BTO plugs in my book. I told him that I very much appreciated twenty-five years of incredible entertainment, and that it was an honor to call him my friend. He smiled, and as he walked away, he looked back at me and said, "When it's all said and done, Ed, friends are the best gift you can ever receive. They outlast records and books."

I smiled and thought about how simple, yet profound, his statement was. And the thing was, he was totally right. I nodded my agreement to him, he smiled, and we both walked away.

There wasn't much time to wax reflective on the night's events as we all had to get some sleep and hustle back to Macon early the next morning. We rode up the elevator one last time and walked into our room. Ray and Hugh immediately took showers and jumped into one of the beds. I took mine right after they did and walked out towards the other one.

When I walked out of the shower, the simple sight of seeing Ray and Hugh in bed together was enough to convulse me into hysterical laughter. Ray was all rolled up on one of his sides like a bear. Hugh was laying on his back, a pensive look on his face somewhat similar to that of a new bride awaiting a dismal wedding night experience. I laughed so hard that Ray said, "E. you might want to play the television loud. Foskey is gonna be barkin' like a plantation dog in a few minutes."

This got me howling to the extent that I almost doubled over in laughter. At this point, Hugh mentioned that he didn't brush his teeth, and needed to go do that. As he did, Ray remarked, "That's good, cause I don't want no bad breath breezin' my balls."

Hugh and I fell over at this. As Hugh slowly calmed down, he finally walked inside the bathroom to brush his teeth. I figured it was now time to get some much-needed rest. As I proceeded to get into my bed, the phone began ringing. Because I happened to be standing right next to it, I picked it up on the first ring.

I put the receiver to my ear and heard a distinctly Canadian-sounding voice say, "Ed, how is the sleeping situation working out down there?" It was Robin!

I replied, "Man, they're in bed together, but as of now they're just engaging in light verbal foreplay."

"Ed, I know it's hard on you to witness stuff like this as I can tell you're almost saintly. As your friend, I would invite you up to my room to escape it, but then you and I would be in a room together, and God forbid that. I can handle groupies, but sleeping with a member of the Brotherhood in the same room—the earth as we know it is not ready for that."

I laughed and agreed. Robin tried one last time to persuade us to come to Myrtle Beach with the band the next day. He said playing the

House of Blues would be great, and that we could all check out the choicest strip clubs in Myrtle Beach afterwards.

I thanked Robin and told him we all wanted to, but that Hugh was a pussy and had to be home the next day. Robin said that he could almost see the umbilical cord that ran between Hugh and Rosemary when he first met him. I told Robin that not only did it run between them, but that it was larger than a reticulated python. We both laughed one last time, promised to keep in touch, and said our goodbyes.

The next morning, Ray, Hugh, and I made our way back to Georgia. We relived the events of the previous night more than one time, and we all laughed and had the best time together. As more miles passed by and the first late morning beer cans were opened, Ray and Hugh looked over at me and said, "This was the best road trip, ever. Thanks, E."

I smiled, and thanked them right back. They are my brothers, you know . . . .

Epilogue

Hey everyone,
I hope y'all enjoyed this, my second book. I had a great time writing it, and I hope you can sense that in the material.

One thing I've enjoyed is working with the staff at River City Publishing. They're cool, and it's been a great experience for me to work with a cover designer, publicist, and editor. My first book basically was printed just as it came off my computer, so it's been real nice to have some professional help with this one. I don't know if I will ever be able to thank Nancy, Tangela, or Ashley enough.

Now, let's get to the meat of things. When you write somewhat wild stuff like I do, you have this tendency to maybe get a little too wild sometimes. A little too "over the line." Maybe even a little too crazy. I've been guilty of this more than once, and I was certainly guilty during the writing of this book.

That being said, I need to tell y'all that one chapter I wrote for this book was deemed a little too wild for the mainstream audience we hope to attract. It was the view of the staff at River City, and I agreed with them. Even so, I'm a democratic sort of guy, and I want the people who read and like my stuff to have the opportunity to read anything they want to. So, here's an offer. The title of the banned chapter is "Sally the Screamer," and it tells of an amorous encounter between Ed Jr. and a lady. More specifically, it's Ed Jr. telling Ray, Hugh, and me about this encounter, so the chapter is written like Ed Jr. is telling the story to us. Which is what actually happened. Anyway, if y'all are interested in reading it, just send me an email at: ed3@ed-williams.com. I will gladly email the "Sally the Screamer" chapter to you.

Once again, many thanks for reading this book, and for your support. It's appreciated more than you know.

Ed